Christian India

CHRISTIAN INDIA

INTRODUCTION BY
Father Trevor Huddleston

TEXT BY
F. A. Plattner

PHOTOGRAPHS BY
B. Moosbrugger

The Vanguard Press
NEW YORK

Translated from the German by
Mollie Seton-Karr

Produced by Thames and Hudson Ltd London and Atlantis Verlag Zürich
Text printed in Great Britain by Jarrold and Sons Ltd Norwich
Photogravure pages printed in France by Braun et Cie Mulhouse

Contents

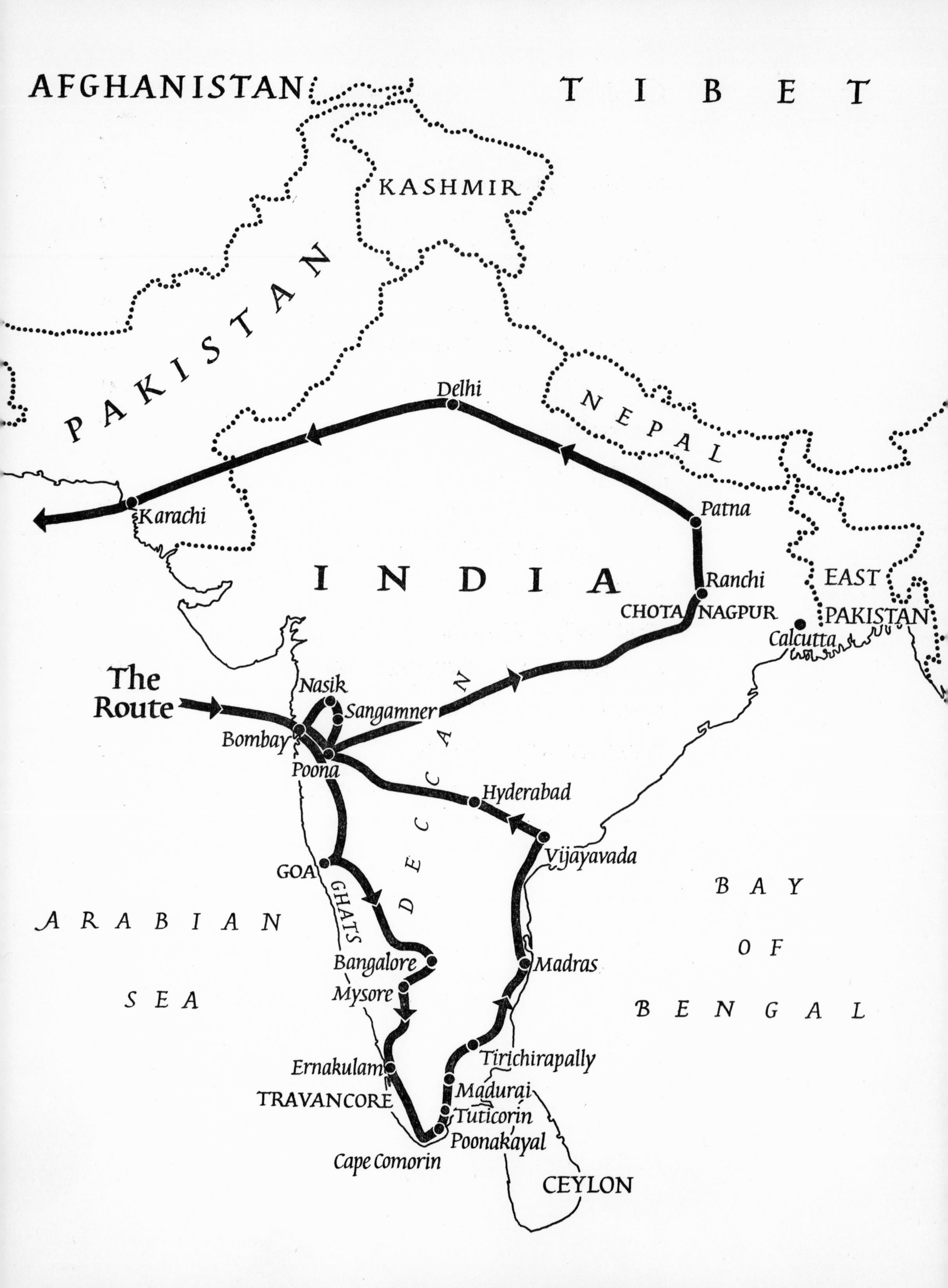
AFGHANISTAN
TIBET
KASHMIR
PAKISTAN
NEPAL
Delhi
Karachi
Patna
INDIA
Ranchi
CHOTA NAGPUR
EAST PAKISTAN
Calcutta
The Route
Nasik
Sangamner
Bombay
Poona
DECCAN
Hyderabad
Vijayavada
GOA
GHATS
ARABIAN SEA
BAY OF BENGAL
Bangalore
Mysore
Madras
Tirichirapally
Ernakulam
TRAVANCORE
Madurai
Tuticorin
Poonakayal
Cape Comorin
CEYLON

Introduction

One of the most fascinating aspects of all missionary work throughout history is the ability of the Church to take root, to grow and to blossom in any soil. The very fact that, in her origin, "Parthians and Medes and Elamites, and the dwellers in Mesopotamia, and in Judaea, and Cappadocia, in Pontus, and Asia, Phrygia and Pamphylia, in Egypt and in the parts of Libya about Cyrene, and strangers of Rome, Jews and proselytes, Cretes and Arabians" all spoke "the wonderful works of God" (Acts ii. vv. 9–11), was a Divine hint of what would be. And the fact also that, at the end of time, "the nations of them which are saved shall walk in the light of it . . . and they shall bring the glory and honour of the nations into it" is proof of the very nature of the Catholic Church herself.

But in the time-process, in this world, between the sowing of the seed and its final harvesting, there stretches a span of history—no one knows how long. And it is that which we can watch in one country and another: it is that which we can actually see developing and changing before our eyes. Nowhere is it more wonderful, more fascinating than in India.

It seems to me that there you have some at least of the most significant processes in the development of the Christian Church plainly visible and comprehensible. You have, first, its impact upon the more ancient civilization of the old India: and the impact upon it of the outward and visible forms of Eastern religion. You have, secondly, that which is equally significant in Africa and in the Far East, the interplay of nationalist and religious interests: often finding expression in racial bitterness or the pride of the traditionalist. And you have, finally, that which is common to the whole world but which in India (and Asia generally) has a sharp and definite form—the sudden contact between an old culture and a brash new technological revolution. In this last process, the old religions as well as Christianity itself are equally involved.

This book, with some of the finest photography ever produced on the subject, sets out to show historically and factually how the Catholic Church has in fact taken root in India; what fruit it already produces; where its peculiar, God-given strength lies.

And indeed a glance through the photographs will indicate immediately and with immense effectiveness—just what has happened: the creation (of course on a small scale, for Christianity in India is very much a minority religion) of a noticeably Christian Indian civilization: unmistakably Christian—unmistakably Indian too.

And the text tells us, very simply and with no attempt at anything more than an outline, the story of Christian Catholic missionary work down the centuries from St Thomas the Apostle to the present time.

The two 'great' periods of Indian missionary endeavour were indeed the very early and the Counter-Reformation periods: the time of the founding of the Syro-Malabar Church in Travancore nineteen hundred years ago, and the coming of that greatest of all Indian missionaries, St Francis Xavier. It is in South India still that the greatest concentration of Christians is to be found—and it is well to remind ourselves that, after nearly two thousand years, there are only some ten million Christians of *all* denominations in the whole of the sub-continent: roughly three per cent of the total population.

*

It would be impertinent for me—and quite unnecessary—to recapitulate any of the story. And the photography is so uniformly excellent that it would be a mistake to single out any particular example for comment.

Rather I would like to stress one or two points which seem to me to be of application more generally, and of crucial importance too.

It becomes obvious, as one reads this book, that the Christian Church has made a contribution, out of all proportion to its size, in the field of education and of social welfare: that, in fact, India like Africa really owes the initiative in all educational effort to the missionary. Today, of course, the control of education has passed from the hands of the Missions to the State: social services, whilst likely to be more slowly secularized in their entirety, are likewise passing. But, parallel to these changes—inevitable and permanent as they must be—is the change which has taken place, and is continuing, within the hierarchy of the Church herself: the gradual replacement of the European 'missionary' priest and bishop and cardinal, with his Indian brother. In other words, the Christian Church in India has reached a point in her history when she must learn to function purely and simply as a Province of the Church Universal—Indian in every fibre of her being, but, essentially and fundamentally, the *Catholic* Church.

That the Church in India, surrounded as she is and must be by the temples and mosques of Hindu and Moslem, will not only survive but make an even greater contribution, there can be no question. But she will have to pass through tribulation, no doubt. It seems to me that the crisis for Christian 'missionary' churches lies here: in their recognition immediately of the forces of an emergent, virile nationalism, and in their adaptability to these new forces.

And it seems to me that there can be but one way of adaptation: the way that Christ Himself showed us in His birth and in His death: *Identification* and *Sacrifice*.

These two words should be the watchwords for the Church in India and in Africa today. For a failure in either can mean the set-back, for generations, of evangelism.

By these words I mean: the readiness of the Christian Church to enter into as fully as possible the whole social fabric in which she is set; the refusal to live in an ivory-tower; the determination to share in the blood and the sweat and the tears of an emerging civilization.

And with this, the readiness to lose her life that she may find it: to be stripped of all that which might hold her tied down to 'Western' ways of thought and expression: of all false values imposed by custom (whether, as in India the caste-system or as in Africa the colour-bar): the readiness to "shed the love of God abroad" at all costs—and it *must* be costly: whether it is wanted or not.

Here is a book which, whilst describing the past and the present, points us to the future. May it be widely read, and deeply understood.

Trevor Huddleston, C.R.

Mirfield
November 5th, 1956

Author's Preface

INDIA is as large as Europe without Russia. It is virtually a continent united in a single state. Few people are likely to have either the time or the desire to motor through the Indian countryside, and drive along the dusty, apparently endless Indian roads, far from the all too rare hotels. Yet this is the only way in which the real life of India is revealed to the traveller. He will see the little villages and hamlets where three-quarters of the 325 million Indians still spend their lives. I myself would have hardly had the courage to embark on such a motor trip with my travelling companion and photographer, Bernhard Moosbrugger of Zurich, had I not cherished the hope that we would find a kindly welcome for our nights on the road in the homes of Catholic priests.

We often tried our faithful *Opel-Kombi* car very severely, driving it at twenty-five miles an hour for ten hours or more at a stretch, over roads in which motor buses and heavy lorries had hammered out ruts. We used to drive along, looking expectantly at each milestone we reached as if it were sure to mark the beginning of a better stretch of road. But, alas, all too often it heralded one in an even worse state. It all depended on whether the road-mender had done his work properly or negligently just filled in the holes.

Though we had chosen the coolest time of the year, from November to the end of February and beginning of March, the midday sun blazed down mercilessly. Between six and seven in the evening the sudden fall of night forced us to call a halt sooner than we would have wished. Often the only food we had from morning until we reached our journey's end in the evening consisted of a few bananas bought in some village.

I should like to take this opportunity of expressing my deep gratitude for the great hospitality with which we, two complete strangers, were received by priests in their poor presbyteries or mission stations. They never failed to make us welcome. We also enjoyed the privilege of being graciously received by several Indian bishops.

In 1946–7 I had travelled widely in India. My new journey was designed on quite a different plan. I wished to obtain a picture of Christian life in the new India, and at the same time I was anxious to participate as a pilgrim in the jubilee celebrations marking the 400th anniversary of the death of St Francis Xavier, and also the 1,900th anniversary of the arrival of the Apostle Thomas in Southern India. Thus our route was planned to retrace the steps of Catholic missionaries in ancient days and in more recent times.

After short visits to Karachi and Ahmedabad I met Bernhard Moos-brugger in Bombay, and together we travelled across part of the Deccan, and established our headquarters with the Swiss Mission of the Society of Jesus in Poona. We then headed south and pushed on towards Goa, where in December 1952 large numbers of Indian Catholics had gathered at the sarcophagus of St Francis Xavier. Turning back to the Deccan we travelled south to Bangalore, Mysore and Coimbatore, whence the exquisitely beautiful Malabar coast, land of the Thomas-Christians, is easily reached through the Palghat pass. By mid-January 1953 we stood on Cape Comorin, the most southerly point of India; then turned northwards, travelling along the Coromandel coast. Tuticorin, Madurai, the health resort of Kodaikanal, Tiruchirapally, Madras and Vijayavada on the lower reaches of the Kistna river were the most important stopping places on our journey. We had a somewhat longer stay in the Jesuit Seminary of Tiruchirapally, where I found a great deal of material to record; and we were also able to enjoy a week's holiday in the admirable care of the Sisters of St Anne from Lucerne at their magnificent hospital in Vijayavada. Driving across Hyderabad we were back at our headquarters in Poona by mid-February; and we witnessed the rapturous welcome which the first Indian Cardinal received in his See of Bombay.

The sequence of our photographs and the accompanying text does not follow the itinerary of our journey. The reason for this is that the order is intended to illustrate the historical development of the Christian Church in India. Christianity has attempted to acquire ascendancy in India at three widely separated periods. The first occasion was in Apostolic days when the Church of the Syro-Malabars or Thomas-Christians was founded in the southernmost part of the sub-continent. The second time was when Catholic missionaries appeared on the west coast at the period of the Portuguese *conquistadores* in the sixteenth to the eighteenth centuries. They made Goa the centre of their activities which extended throughout Asia. Finally, in the days of the British Empire, and especially since the middle of the last century, a strong Protestant missionary movement took place. This was the time of the great expansion of the city of Bombay, the gateway to India, and the work of the missionaries ceased to be restricted to the west coast and part of the south, but slowly spread over the whole country from the Himalayas to Cape Comorin, and from burning Quetta in Baluchistan to the damp mist-shrouded hills of Assam.

To this day Christianity in India exhibits clear traces of the three contrasting epochs of ideological penetration from which it has sprung. In the text and the photographs of this book we have attempted to present the different characteristics of these three religious and cultural groups of Indian Christians. Though we are far from having exhausted the subject, we hope that we have succeeded in giving an over-all impression of the whole picture of Christian India as it is at the present day. Our photographs have been chosen in order to make the Indian background, which has been depicted in so many books, play but a small part; indeed, to act merely as the accompaniment to our principal theme.

In depicting Christian India we feel that, as two grateful pilgrims, we have produced a new, and perhaps not unrewarding, work.

*

The exact meaning of *Christian India* must be examined. Our title must not mislead anyone into thinking that India is a country with a Christian outlook. The members of all the Christian communions in the sub-continent amount to ten million, which is barely three per cent of the whole population. Yet an independent Christianity does exist in India, and this is what we have tried to present to our readers. There is also another point which we must make clear. As the foregoing indicates, we travelled in the steps of the Catholic missions, and our photographs are concerned with their work only, though the text does also refer to the activities of the Protestant missions. The restricted scope of our survey must in no way be taken to suggest that the achievements of the Evangelical missions are not as equally deserving of praise as those of the Catholic missions. The time at our disposal did not allow us to visit the various centres of their work; and the fact that the Protestant Church is split into many different groups makes a general survey of its activities somewhat difficult to achieve. Thus it is with no desire to belittle the beliefs of our Evangelical fellow-Christians and the selfless work of their missionaries that I repeat that our survey is limited to a description of Roman Catholic activities.

We are extremely grateful to Dr Martin Hürlimann, whose suggestion it was that the author and the photographer team up together. He it was also who selected the hundred photographs reproduced from some three thousand taken by Bernhard Moosbrugger.

Felix Alfred Plattner

3

On Cape Comorin

THE peninsula of India, its base in the Asiatic mainland, juts out like a great wedge to divide the waters of the two southern oceans. Its most southerly point, whose rocky cliffs thrust themselves into the blazing tropical sea, is called Cape Comorin. The name is derived from the Goddess Kumari, and the spot is sacred to Indians. Numerous pilgrims make their way along the dusty roads leading to the cape in order to take a purifying bath to wash away their sins at the confluence of the waters of the two oceans. The narrow belt of land at Cape Comorin is the junction of the two climatic zones which give the Indian landscape its dual character. It is here that the geological reason for the contrast between the eastern and the western halves of India—namely the Ghats—forces itself on the attention of the visitor. This chain of mountains runs through the entire body of the peninsula like a backbone. On the steep ridges of the western side of the range, thick clouds driven by the monsoon discharge a heavy rainfall. "The mountains milk the clouds," say the local peasants.

This accounts for the lush tropical vegetation which characterizes the comparatively narrow coastal strip of the Konkan, and Malabar. From Bombay via Goa, Mangalore and Cochin, almost as far as Cape Comorin, stretches an uninterrupted garden of superb coconut palms. There is no lack of fresh greenery in this region. The aspect of the much wider plain to the east of the Ghats is strikingly different. Here the high plateau of the Deccan slopes slowly and gradually towards the shores of the flat coast. It is a dry and thirsty land, often subject to drought, and dependent on artificial irrigation, water being drawn from wide rivers and lakes where the rainfall has been conserved.

Near Cape Comorin, the dramatic change in the character of the landscape takes place suddenly within a few miles. Shortly after quitting the richly fertile Malabar coast, the traveller reaches the foot of the 'Mountain of the Healing Herbs'; and no sooner has he entered the low pass leading to the

1. *Fishing village on Cape Comorin*
2. *The last spurs of the Ghats under a stormy sky*
3. *Row of huge terra-cotta horses in front of a small temple in the country near Madurai*
4. *'The Mountain of the Healing Herbs'*

Tinevelly district than he is faced with the prospect of a vast arid waste, whose only vegetation consists of sparse and slender toddy-palms, their tall trunks topped by small bushy bunches of leaves which provide an enchanting spectacle.

Late one afternoon towards the end of January we left Nagercoil, the most southerly town in India, by car; and within half an hour's drive, the last spurs of the Ghats lay behind us. A few stray clouds, aftermath of a recent thunderstorm, still hung on the mountain cliffs, and the slanting rays of the setting sun shone through their haze. But above our heads stretched the uncompromisingly blue dome of the sky from which, even in the rainy season, few refreshing showers seemed likely to fall.

The whole of India is subject to, and conditioned by, the unalterable cycle of the monsoons, which provide or deny the life-giving rain to the parched, thirsty tropical land. This fact helps one to understand the gloomy fatalism of the peasants, and the glowing faith which they bring to the worship of their gods. The mythical world of idols conceived by the imagination of the dark-skinned South Indian people, who are of Dravidian blood, fills our Western minds with horror. It is a world of demons, in which animals are deified, and gods turned into beasts, snakes and elephants, horses and apes, while birds and ants are transformed into mysterious symbols of mythological powers which, in turn, assume human shape to dominate men's destinies. Yet all the while these beings themselves remain in thrall to complicated laws, and are enmeshed in the fatalistic cycle of a never-ending round of birth, life, and fading away.

5. *Boat with a load of coconuts on the Quilon lagoon*

6. *Fishermen's nets at the entrance to the harbour of Cochin*

7. *Landscape of palm trees in Malabar*

5

6

Beneath the Palms of Malabar

MALABAR is one of the most beautiful regions of India, and, as it is extremely fertile, it is also one of the most densely populated. The coconut palms are the chief characteristic of the landscape, and indeed these superb trees with their prolific foliage are the land's main source of wealth. Every single part of them is of practical value. The nut itself yields a nourishing and refreshing milk. The kernel or copra has a high oil content. Fresh copra can be used for domestic purposes; when dried it forms the basis for the manufacture of vegetable fats, edible oil and soap. The natives make household utensils out of the hard shells, and also use them to produce carved souvenirs for sale to tourists. The bark can be processed to form stout rope and matting; and many a person has slept soundly on a 'horsehair' mattress blissfully unaware that the 'hair' has grown on a coconut. The trunks of the trees provide invaluable material for building houses, and are used in the construction of the streamlined skiffs which cruise ceaselessly along canals of dreamlike beauty and on enchanting lagoons. The Malabar peasant lives in the shade of his palm trees, and the entire length of the coast is dotted with massed congeries of his rustic huts. The merchants and the craftsmen, on the other hand, congregate in numerous villages and small townships. Farther inland, where the hilly zone begins, the palm trees are gradually replaced by rice-fields, and still farther from the coast, on the escarpments of the Ghats, an area of tropical woodland is reached.

No Malabar village is without a Hindu temple. Both the architecture and the religion seem to have developed so as to harmonize with the lush prodigality of the natural surroundings. One day, on hearing the dull drone of temple drums, we interrupted our journey. Leaving the car we painfully climbed on to the bastion of the temple walls to behold three mighty elephants, on whose backs stood dark-skinned natives waving bunches of dazzlingly white feathers and round, multi-coloured fans, in time to the rhythmic beat of the tom-toms. The elephants' magnificent head ornaments glittered in golden glory; and in a large shady hall devout Indians swarmed round the musicians who handled their drums with great skill, beating them in perfect time. An inexplicable fascination emanated from this magical music. Although the sound and the surroundings are so entirely different, I can only compare it with the emotion which one feels on listening to the church

8. Coolie with a load of baskets at Ernakulam

bells pealing at home. Meanwhile the Brahmin priests, who had withdrawn into a small inner sanctum, out of the sight of the crowds, were presenting the offerings for the *Pooja* (Hindu worship).

One of the best known temples in Malabar is that of Ettumanur, not far from Kottayam. As we were not allowed to enter the building we could only catch a brief glimpse of its marvellous interior. Like most of the places of Hindu worship in India, Ettumanur is constructed of wood. Only the outer walls, which enclose large courtyards, extensive quarters for pilgrims, houses for the Brahmin priests, and other structures, are built of stone. The steeply pitched roofs, designed to protect the upper storeys from the tropical downpours which occur in the rainy season, are the outstanding features of the building. This architectural feature is also to be found in Nepal.

Concrete proof of the enormously rich gifts which the Hindu pilgrim centres receive is provided by the immense decorative flagpole which guards the holy of holies, where, withdrawn in a mystic twilight, the image of the god is enthroned. The entire surface of this huge piece of teak—the termite-proof wood—is veneered with sheets of solid gold; and one of the Brahmin priests, when in conversation with us, proudly alluded to a considerable hoard of gold and jewels which is concealed, or rather buried, within the precincts of the temple.

9. Elephants caparisoned for a ceremony in a temple at Trichur, Malabar

10. Entrance to the temple of Ettumanur, near Kottayam

11. Brahmin children at Ettumanur

On the Holy Hill of the Thomas-Christians

THIS unique country, whose long stretch of fertile coast lies open to the western seas, is the home of one of the oldest and most interesting Christian communities in existence. When we visited Malabar, at the end of December 1952, this Church was preparing to celebrate, in accordance with its proud and immemorial tradition, the 1,900th anniversary of its foundation by the Apostle St Thomas. I can still hear the voice of the Archbishop of Ernakulam, in his capacity as Metropolitan of the Syro-Malabar Catholics, saying in answer to the Papal Cardinal-Legate who had just presented his credentials, "You come from Peter; and we are the sons of another Apostle—Thomas."

Modern research is inclined to accept as true the traditional claim of the Travancore Christians to have been evangelized by St Thomas. Ever since the Romans conquered Egypt in the year 30 B.C., the importance of the commercial sea route to India via the Red Sea has been recognized. It was the pilot Hippalus who discovered what great assistance the trade winds offer to ships crossing the Indian Ocean. In consequence trade began to flourish, and never again until the nineteenth century did this route carry so great a volume of shipping. During the reign of Nero, though the economic situation in Rome was dangerously precarious, the exchange of gold for the pepper of Malabar, and the trade in precious stones from India, and Chinese silks, seems to have reached a peak. The positions of the chief ports on the Malabar coast were well known to Greek and Roman geographers of the period. Muziris, now known as Cranganore, was the most prosperous of the Indian trading centres. It then stood on the estuary formed by Malabar backwaters which entered the sea at that spot. They have since changed their courses, and now flow towards Cochin, thus depriving Muziris of its importance as a harbour for sea-going ships.

It is, therefore, quite possible that the Apostle Thomas could have come to India, perhaps with the intention of converting the Jewish communities known to have been established there. According to tradition he erected seven 'crosses' or churches in Malabar, and was later martyred in Mylapore, which is now a suburb of Madras. Reliable records exist about the place of his martyrdom, although they only date from the sixth century. Mediaeval travellers, such as Marco Polo and Giovanni di Montecorvino, agree that an

12. Worshippers leaving the church at Kuravilangad after attending early Mass

old church still existed in Malabar in their time, and was then in the keeping of a small Christian community. In 1523 excavations were carried out on that spot by an official Portuguese mission. Under the altar, at a depth of several feet, a tomb containing human remains was discovered. Among other finds was a stone on which two figures had been roughly carved. One of these undoubtedly represents St Thomas, who is depicted holding the Gospels in one hand, while the fingers of the other are extended as if ready to be thrust into the wound in Christ's side, according to the account given by St John the Evangelist in his Gospel. In 1547 further excavations were carried out in the chapel, which local tradition believes to stand on the spot where the Saint was martyred—a hill some six miles south-west of Madras. Here the Portuguese found a cross bearing a Pahlevi inscription, which, on reliable authority, can be assigned to the seventh century. A similar cross, which came originally from the Valliapally Church, near Kottayam, bears an almost identical inscription, which has not yet been completely deciphered.

Whatever the historical accuracy of these ancient traditions may be, the fact remains that the Syro-Malabar religious communities are of very early Christian origin. This is definitely confirmed by the travel diaries kept by the Byzantine monk, Kosmos Indikopleustes, the Indian Wayfarer, who made journeys in the sub-continent in A.D. 535. It is now accepted as a fact that at the time of the persecutions of the Christians by Sapor II of Persia (A.D. 345) a merchant named Thomas Kana, accompanied by a considerable retinue of followers, came to Cranganore, where he was granted various privileges by the local ruler. Records of official concessions to Christians, engraved on copper plates during the eighth or ninth century, are preserved to this day in the churches of Kothurutti and Muttam.

The first contacts between the Thomas-Christians and the bishops of Mesopotamia date from about this period and, as time went on, these bonds were strengthened. In spite of occasional interruptions the links have been maintained until the present time, and they throw considerable light on the subject of the religious rites of the Indian Catholic Church. Its priests use the antique Syrian idiom as their liturgic language, and its ceremonies have definite kinship with those of the so-called Chaldean rite of Babylon and Seleucia near Baghdad.

The early history of these remote Christian churches is difficult to follow clearly. Although the information is scanty we can safely infer that Christian communities were established—possibly intermittently—all along India's west coast, from Bombay to Cape Comorin. Their parent settlement, however, lay south of the Ponani river, near the Palghat pass, and extended as far as Quilon. The seat of their religious leader was in Ernakulam.

The individual manner in which this section of Christendom developed is of special interest, for it grew and flourished entirely uninfluenced by the evolution, or affected by the schisms, of the Mediterranean churches; and stood firm against the tremendous power of its Hindu neighbours. When the Portuguese landed in India about 1500, they estimated that the number of Thomas-Christian families was 30,000, which suggested a total of some 120,000 to 150,000 souls. Most of these people had settled inland and lived by agriculture or by trading in pepper and coconuts. Like their Hindu neighbours, they belonged to the Dravidian race, though some of them showed, and still show, in their appearance traces of Semitic blood. Socially they formed a well integrated group, able to maintain their rights by a display of military power, and ready, if necessary, to take arms against the rival rulers surrounding them, who were frequently engaged in internecine strife.

Thomas-Christians also enjoyed a position of high rank in the caste-system of India. This was undoubtedly due to the antiquity of the Christian communities, for they were already well established when the caste-system stiffened to the iron rigidity which it attained in Malabar. Otherwise the Syro-Malabar Christians would never have obtained the high rank which they still enjoy. Moreover, the fact that they accepted the Indians' social structure may well account for the preservation of Syro-Malabar Christianity with all its peculiar characteristics.

There are also indications that the Thomas-Christians, out of a desire for self-preservation or on account of a rather unworthy feeling of superiority, were inclined to avoid choosing their converts from the lowest classes of the population. In fact the Syro-Malabar Christians are, to this day, divided into two distinct social groups, whose members would no more consider contracting a marriage with each other than would members of different Hindu castes. Today it is extremely difficult to establish the origin of this cleavage. According to popular tradition, the more aristocratic group is descended from the children of Thomas Kana by his legitimate wife, whereas the lower section trace their origin to his progeny by a concubine. The truth would appear to be that the inferior group belonged from the start to Hindu families of low caste—they may even have been Untouchables—who were not allowed even by conversion to rise to a higher rank. Whatever the reason may be, the social difference between the two groups is maintained to this day, and is so strong that the Church is obliged to accept it and to attune its attitude to the established situation. To avoid possible ill-feeling and ensure peaceful conditions each group has been granted separate bishops and priests, who are chosen from their respective ranks.

It is interesting to note that a similar division is to be found among the

Roman Catholics of Latin rite in Travancore. Here the separation was originally due to the difference in caste among the population of fisher folk; and it is the reason why the diocese of Cochin is split into two. These facts illustrate the tolerance of popular opinion which the Syro-Malabar Church was obliged to display in shaping its organization, and in carrying out its mission to care for men's souls. It is therefore not surprising to learn that when the Portuguese missionaries first came into contact with the Thomas-Christians in the sixteenth century, grave misunderstandings arose bearing the seeds of future serious trouble.

From the religious point of view the Syro-Malabars were true Christians, and had kept their faith pure. They believed in the Trinity, in the Holy Incarnation, and in our Lord and Saviour Jesus Christ; in the Church with its hierarchy; in the sacraments and in the future life. They celebrated Mass, acknowledged Baptism, the Holy Eucharist and the ordination of priests as sacraments; accepted the remission of sins through confession and the Extreme Unction for the dying; and made their vows for indissoluble marriage before a priest. Christmas, the Epiphany, Easter and Whitsuntide were celebrated as Church Feasts; worship of the Cross was much observed, but though they honoured Our Lady and the Saints, no images stood in their simple churches, which were built of wood.

Thus the essence of the Christian Faith had been preserved by the Syro-Malabar Church, and the morals of its members were praised by Portuguese missionaries. But they found that church attendance had become very slack, that the teaching imparted to the people was poor, and that a number of superstitious practices were prevalent. Nevertheless, the Thomas-Christians immediately acknowledged the arrival of the Portuguese in India, the priests of the Latin rite came into touch with them, and entered into ecclesiastical communion, the Indian Christians being ready to recognize the authority of the Pope and the Bishop of Goa.

As might have been expected, the gradual incorporation of the Syro-Malabar Christians into the organization of the Church of Rome was not carried out without difficulties. No problems of dogma arose, though questions of discipline, rite and duties had to be settled; and political and economic factors also played an important part in the discussions. In 1599 the representatives of all Syro-Malabar communities accepted an Edict of the Synod of Udiamperur, near Cochin. From the point of view of dogma, the edict condemned certain signs of Nestorian influence, whereas in regard to the ritual of the church it ordained a strict adherence to the decisions of the Council of Trent, thus introducing a liturgy which followed the use of Rome with almost exaggerated conformity. Even drastic innovations such as a celibate priesthood and individual confession of sins were accepted, and conscientiously carried out. This energetic intervention on the part of the bishops of Goa and their main assistants, the Jesuit missionaries, is explained by the state of neglect into which the Syro-Malabar religious body had fallen.

But in accordance with the bigoted spirit of their time, the Jesuits failed to appreciate the natural peculiarities of the Indian-Christian communities with whom they had to deal. This led to misunderstandings, and finally to a schism which occurred in 1653, over fifty years after the Edict of the Synod. The titular head of the Syro-Malabar Churches was an archdeacon, on whom all ecclesiastical nominations depended. This enviable position had become practically a hereditary right in one family, which naturally feared to lose its power should the jurisdiction of the Bishop of Cochin be recognized. The archdeacon therefore attempted to convoke an assembly of Syrian church dignitaries, most of whom virtually depended on him for their nominations. The schismatic Archbishop of Antioch answered the appeal of the archdeacon, who eventually fell under the influence of his unorthodox faction, accepted its Nestorian beliefs and, in consequence, ceased to be a faithful son of the Church of Rome. He and his followers were the originators of the sect which became known as the Jacobites, and at present has some 600,000 adherents. In the nineteenth century a section joined the Anglican Church and became known as 'Reformed Jacobites' or 'Mar-Thomites'. These now number 200,000 souls in their communion.

The number of Syro-Malabar Christians remaining faithful to the Church of Rome reached the total of over a million souls in the course of time, and today they form an important religious community, with two archbishoprics and six dioceses. They have preserved Syrian as their liturgical language, although efforts are being made at the present time to replace it by the native tongue Malayalam. The religious observances of the people, and the public ceremonial in connection with ecclesiastical life and worship, however, follow the model of the Latin Church very faithfully. This influence is of very ancient origin, and is displayed in ecclesiastical architecture as early as the seventeenth century. Syro-Malabar churches of that period indeed hardly differ from those built about the same time in the communities established on the coast by Portuguese missionaries. In some instances an elegant, whitewashed Baroque façade has been built on to a nave of pre-Portuguese date. This type of building is also to be found in Jacobite districts, as their churches were erected or modified when the community was strictly Roman Catholic, before the schism of 1653.

The Thomas-Christians preferred to build their sanctuaries on hilltops, and they stand out high above the palm trees in whose shade villages and farms lie hidden. One of the loveliest positions is that of the church at Kuravilangad, near Kottayam. This large village was the home of the 'de Campos' Varghese family which produced many influential archdeacons. It lapsed into schism, but returned to the fold of Rome together with some thirty other communities when Shandi (Chandy) or Alexander de Campos was appointed bishop in 1663.

We arrived in Kuravilangad on a Friday morning after sunrise. At this early hour worshippers were already climbing the magnificent wide staircase leading to the church. On arrival on the spacious landing at the top, many people prayed to the Cross which stands there; and some lit small votive oil lamps which would remain burning in token of their devotion. After the close of the service the crowd silently left the all-too-small church, with its gay, many-coloured Baroque altars, at the very moment when the first rays of the sun filtered through the leaves of the palm trees. The white garments in which the Malabars are wont to drape themselves shone dazzlingly in the bright morning light. Then, after early worship, these men and women all walked quietly down to the village to begin their daily work. At night the mother always gathers the whole family round her for evening prayers, in accordance with the old, faithfully observed Thomas-Christian custom.

Although they are so steeped in tradition Syro-Malabar Christians are at the same time amazingly progressive. Just as they have succeeded in acquiring great importance in the economic field, so they are also the best educated and most advanced people in the whole of the Travancore-Cochin state. Not only does practically every parish possess its elementary school, but the administration also finances 120 secondary schools, 105 intermediary schools and seven university colleges. Many Christians educated in these institutions feel the call to take Holy Orders or join a brotherhood. The Syro-Malabars have, therefore, more than sufficient priests and nuns for their own parochial and diocesan needs, and a great many of them are now active all over South India, some acting as missionaries and priests in the rare Christian communities of the north. It is estimated that the number of these workers amounts to some 400 priests, 200 monks and 500 nuns.

Until now all priests working outside their native dioceses have had, on entering sees of the Latin rite, to give up their own Syro-Malabar rite. This renunciation of their own traditional cult not only appears to those who must make it a great personal sacrifice, but it is also considered by some Thomas-Christian leaders to be a most painful loss to their own religious community. They consider that their centuries'-old tradition entitles them to call themselves the *first-born* Indian Christians, and feel that they have specially deep links with all Indian peoples. Moreover, they believe that their own rite and forms of worship are better suited to Oriental mentalities than the more formal ceremonial of the Roman-Latin cult. This explains why they find it so very painful to see the ancient and honoured Church of the Thomas-Christians denied the right to found new missions outside the narrow limits of its present jurisdiction, which is restricted to the small Travancore-Cochin district. On the other hand, those endowed with deeper insight cannot fail to realize that, going by past experience, it is dangerous to allow different Catholic rites to co-exist in a restricted area, as such a custom may easily produce highly undesirable results.

The problem is not easy to solve. On the one side stand the well-justified endeavours of Rome to maintain peace and harmony. On the other are ranged the new spirit and traditional power of expansion of the Syro-Malabar Church. The dynamic and ever-growing community of the Thomas-Christians possesses great resources which could be put to excellent use in helping the needy Northern and Central Indian dioceses, and trying to bring them in line with the richer and better endowed ones. Modernizing the liturgy might be a helpful step; and it is clear that efforts have recently been made by all joint churches gradually to replace Syrian Latin (in which Mass has been until now celebrated) by the native tongue.

There is no doubt that the Christian Indians, heirs of St Thomas's teaching, can still look forward to a great future. Judging by the example of this distant Church, for so long separated from Rome, one can well realize what a powerful and reviving impetus even the most paralysed members of Christendom can receive from the living head of the Roman Catholic Church —namely his Holiness the Pope.

13. Stone bas-relief representing St Thomas, found in the Apostle's tomb near Mylapore

14. Ancient Syrian cross, dating from the seventh century, in the church at Valliapally

15. Church at Kuravilangad, and the cross which stands before it

16. The priest's house, built in Malabar style, at Kadamattam

17. Baroque façade of a Jacobite church at Kadamattam, with a porch added at a later date

18. Procession of Thomas-Christians bearing silver crosses

13

14

15

16

17

18

With the Fishermen of Travancore

Most of the Thomas-Christians are peasants and merchants living inland, whereas lower down on the coast numerous fishing villages may be found where the rough Mukkavams have their dwelling. One of the most marvellous experiences which a motor journey through India affords is that it enables the traveller to move not only in space but in time. Within a few miles and minutes the tourist drives back into past centuries; shortly after leaving surroundings where the technical achievements of modern civilization are in evidence, he enters a mediaeval, or possibly even a stone-age, world. No sooner has one driven out of Ernakulam or Trivandrum, the capital of Travancore, where the streets are lined with shops filled with the latest novelties, than the sea-shore comes in sight, where fishermen in their *catamarans* glide through the surf to land straight on the beach. Roughly built from lengths of crudely-hewn palm-tree trunks, the design of these boats or rafts has remained unaltered since time immemorial. They have preserved their primitive shape, which does not permit the introduction of any new fishing methods, nor can they venture into deeper waters in search of new fishing grounds which might provide greater quantities of fish for the growing population. The organization of the business does not seem to have improved either. Half the catch belongs to the owner of the net, which is drawn in a semicircle through shallow waters just off-shore; the remainder goes to the men who help with the fishing. The fish is auctioned immediately, on the beach, going to the highest bidder among the women, who then load it on their heads and carry it to the nearest village or township across the dunes.

Everything—the huts, the food, the miserable clothing and the tools which these fishermen use—appears to have remained unchanged since the dawn of time. Thus the modern pilgrim can easily picture to himself the arrival of St Francis Xavier in 1544 on his mission to evangelize the Mukkavams. Accompanied only by a few followers who acted as interpreters, the holy man visited all the villages from Cape Comorin to Quilon, teaching children and adults. He confined his instruction to simple prayers, assured himself of their serious intention to go on living as good Christians, and then baptized the whole flock. Those whom he had thus gained by the power of his Christlike love, he then handed over to the care of his assistants so that they

19. Fisherman mending his nets at Rajakamangulam (Travancore)

might complete and carry on his godly mission. This was the procedure he followed in India and later in Japan.

The memory of Francis Xavier is alive to this day among these Indian Christian fisher-folk. Every village claims to have been individually converted by the saint, and everywhere one is greeted with legends illustrating his personality. The miracles attributed to him are far outside the realm of serious historical criticism. We had the good fortune and great pleasure of being accompanied during the whole of our visit to the Travancore coast by the Jesuit father, P. Schurhammer, one of the leading authorities on St Francis Xavier. Through his remarkable knowledge of the smallest details of the great missionary's life, he was able to discriminate between the truth and the fanciful stories related by the Mukkavams and their Indian priests, who never stopped talking about the saint's miracles, as recorded by local tradition.

One day when we had taken refuge from the heat of the blazing midday sun in the shade of the church at Colachel, four men appeared carrying a young girl who was obviously in a dying condition, in the hope that she might be cured by means of the prayers for healing pronounced by one of the white 'Swamis' dressed in priests' cassocks. Events such as this illustrate how vividly the blessed memory of St Francis is kept alive to this day by the fishermen of Travancore.

20. Fisherman on the coast of Travancore

21. Fishermen returning, Poonakayal

22. Casting the nets in the evening near Marmogao, Goa

20

21

Mar Severios

THE unmistakable spiritual upsurge of the United Thomas-Christians (United to the Church of Rome) has not been completely ignored by the schismatic Jacobites. During the last decade some of their bishops, followed by a number of priests and thousands of members of the Church, have decided to rejoin the Church of Rome. Mar Ivanios was the first who in 1930 rejoined the Mother Church. He was allowed to preserve his West Syrian (Antiochian) rite, provided that it was cleansed from all Nestorian errors, and was allowed to celebrate Mass in the native language of Travancore, that is, the Malayalam tongue. The Pope appointed Mar Ivanios Archbishop of Trivandrum, and at the same time gave him jurisdiction over his religious followers, the so-called 'Syro-Malankara' Christians. His example was followed a few years later by Mar Severios, who until the time of his remarkable conversion had been considered to be one of the most determined and energetic opponents of the Union with Rome movement. He then became one of its most zealous protagonists.

For a whole week we were the guests of Mar Severios in the Bishop's residence at Tiruvalla. This gave us the opportunity of seeing for ourselves what great energy, far-sighted judgment, power of concentration and thoughtfulness this Indian Prince of the Church possessed. In the short span of some fifteen years he brought into being a number of churches and chapels, seven intermediary schools, a teachers' seminary, orphanages and similar institutions. His heart's desire, however, was to bring about the union of his estranged brethren with the Mother Church of Rome. His longing for this was made even stronger because he himself had only returned to the fold after so prolonged a struggle and so much controversy. He tried his physical strength so greatly through working for this goal that his constitution proved unequal to the strain. He died suddenly early in 1955.

On one particular Sunday we accompanied Mar Severios to a distant place inland where he had arranged to celebrate, together with the Jacobites and the Mar-Thomists, a joint Mass in honour of St Thomas. The service was held in an ancient church, and the Christians had assembled round it in their thousands. The bishops drove in procession in a splendidly decorated lorry preceded by drummers, and as they passed along were greeted by jubilant cheers from the crowd.

23. *Mar Severios driving in state to a United Roman Catholic gathering*

The most impressive event of our visit to the Thomas-Christians was, however, the jubilee celebration at Ernakulam. Priests from every parish of Travancore, bearing crosses and blue, red or yellow umbrellas, which are, in this country, a sign of official importance, made their way towards the City of Palms, which was the appointed meeting-place. The Eucharistic procession consisted of tens of thousands of worshippers and hundreds of Indian priests and nuns, who were followed by the bishops, in whose midst walked the Papal Cardinal-Legate. The splendidly decorated streets were lined by Christians and Hindus in their hundreds of thousands; and it would be no exaggeration to say that about 300,000 Catholics were assembled in the large square in which, that morning, High Mass was celebrated according to the Latin, Syro-Malabar and Syro-Malankara rites. All members of the living Indian Catholic Church, though differing in their individual cults, are united in their faith.

24. *Drummers leading a procession*

25. *Mar Severios celebrating High Mass in the Syro-Malabar rite on the occasion of the St Thomas anniversary celebrations in Ernakulam. He is seen at the moment of the Elevation of the Host*

26. *Syro-Malabar sister of the Order of Bethany*

27. *Women kneeling in prayer during the Eucharistic procession at Ernakulam*

Goa or the Expatriate Church

In 1498 Vasco da Gama reached the Indian coast near Calicut. The Portuguese efforts to discover the sea-route to India were thus, after many decades of struggle, crowned with success. When asked for what he was searching on those distant shores, the *conquistador* characteristically replied, "For pepper and souls." Thus the second period of evangelization in India began about 1500.

During the next ten years the Portuguese, by means of bold military operations, conquered all the key positions on the coast of the Indian Ocean in order to ward off Mohammedan incursions and to protect the lucrative trade in spices. As Portugal was a typical maritime power, her colonial policy differed from that followed by the Spaniards in South America. She did not attempt to secure large inland possessions. The activities of the Roman Catholic missionaries were therefore limited to the narrow strip of coast over which the Portuguese ruled.

The spiritual organization of the Church in the Portuguese colonial empire developed in accordance with rules conditioned by mediaeval ideas on the subject of the temporal power of the Representative of Christ on earth. The Pope of the period had, from the earliest days of their conquests, laid on the Kings of Portugal the responsibility for the establishment of the Church "in all lands discovered or still to be discovered" in the Far East. In the name of the crown and with its financial support, parishes for the colonists were created all over the new Lusitanian possessions, and missionaries were sent forth to convert the native population. In 1533 Goa, the capital of the Portuguese colony in India, was chosen as the bishop's see. All missions received their instructions from these headquarters; and it was 'Golden Goa' which imbued them with their peculiar characteristics and gave them the name by which they have been known throughout the centuries.

The evangelization of Goa is inseparably linked with the personality of St Francis Xavier, although he was not the first missionary of the Roman Catholic drive in India. All sixteenth-century missions received their impetus from him, and it was he also who, to a large extent, set the pattern of their spiritual life and material organization. As a Spanish nobleman, he still typified the spirit of the Crusaders, and he would not even have considered the idea of appealing to the 'secular arm' to help him guard the rights of the Church against the 'heathens'. As a disciple of Ignatius de Loyola, he was, however, also the pioneer of a new era. He showed more understanding of, and respect for, foreign ideas and beliefs than had been customary in the past. His weapon was not the sword, but a limitless love of all mankind. This is clearly shown in the numerous letters he wrote to his colleagues exhorting them to Christian charity.

St Francis Xavier landed in Goa in 1542, and immediately founded a seminary for the education of native priests. He then hurried to the Paravas, on the coast inhabited by the fishing folk, south of Madras, in order to give these people, who were Christians in name only, a sounder religious education. He personally baptized the inhabitants of a group of fishermen's villages in Travancore; and then sailed away to the Molucca islands, and still farther on to Japan to open more doors for the entry of Christianity. His daring attempt to reach China was frustrated by his lonely death in December 1552 on a small island off the coast near Hong Kong. Although this great pioneer was allowed only ten years of activity in Asia, his work and his spirit will never be forgotten. He bequeathed them as an example and a legacy to his colleagues and brethren in the East. Everything achieved by the Asiatic missions of Jesuits, Franciscans, Dominicans and Carmelites from the sixteenth to the eighteenth century, was undoubtedly the result of the pioneer work of the far-sighted St Francis Xavier.

The Portuguese missionaries of that period have a lasting achievement to their credit—the evangelization of large parts of the west coast of India, and especially of Goa itself, of Daman which lies farther north; the immediate hinterland of Bombay; and, moving farther south, of Mangalore, Cochin, Quilon, and finally of the coast on either side of Cape Comorin. Here small separate groups of inhabitants were converted; but in order to simplify the story, they can be referred to as 'Goanese', since they all belong to one and the same Church, which has its individual religious rite and depends on Goa for its spiritual and secular guidance. Later some account will be given of another distinct group which came into being in the South Indian district of Madurai.

The religious ceremonies of the Goanese communities clearly reflect the lasting influence of Portuguese forms of worship, which have been preserved since the time of their foundation. In conformity with the watchword *Cuius Regio eius religio* which at that time was accepted throughout Europe, the official Portuguese missions set themselves the task of converting the natives in all the regions where their influence had been established. The Mohammedans, who were then considered the 'hereditary foes' of Christendom, were driven away or massacred; the western Hindus on the other hand were courted; and the Portuguese made every effort to win them over by offering them various political and administrative advantages. Those who continued to show reluctance were made second-grade citizens only. Vice-regal decrees are still in existence which forbid such persons to exercise certain functions, hold state offices, celebrate their religion openly and so forth. The use of force, threats or bodily violence, which had often been practised at the beginning of missionary endeavour, were strictly forbidden by the first Goa Synod held in 1567. The unrestrained methods of the missions, which seem so mistaken to modern Christians, were, however, perfectly correct by sixteenth-century standards.

Arrogantly proud of their military supremacy, and confident in their cultural superiority, the early *conquistadores* and the first missionaries made no attempt to understand or to study the Hindu religion and the manners and customs of the people. They considered the numerous Hindu gods to be repellent, the mythology they found laughable, and the Hindu ritual prohibitions they dismissed as superstitions. The converted Indian had to be completely Europeanized. In the urban districts these native Christians did become thoroughly assimilated with their conquerors; the Portuguese have always, from their first contacts with the Eastern races until the present day, ignored any colour-bar. Thus, owing to intermarriage, the population of the entire colony became a mixed race with marked Indian features. Converts at their baptism were given, as an honour and a 'christening gift', the family names of their god-parents, who were for the most part Portuguese viceroys. The population of Goa still includes many men bearing the names of De Souza, Castro, Braganza, Albuquerque and other proud and ancient Portuguese patronyms.

These new Christians also copied the style of dress of their political masters, the food they ate, and the way of life they followed; and the native language remained the only bond to bind them together as a separate nation. The administration, organization of social life, law and government in Goa were also faithfully copied from those existing in Portugal.

Similar methods of systematic Europeanization were also applied to religious matters. Goa was to become a second Lisbon, with resplendent Baroque churches, stately monasteries and convents, peopled with monks and nuns; church festival days corresponding to those observed in Portugal, marked by processions in honour of the nation's favourite saints, St James, St Sebastian, St Anthony and others much venerated in Lisbon. This foreign spirit slowly penetrated to even the remotest villages visited by the missionaries. Round Salsette the Jesuits introduced the architectural style which is associated with them, and their own saints, whilst in the neighbourhood of Bardiz, ornate little churches still seem to breathe the spirit of the Franciscan monks who built them.

Even the small chapels standing on the dunes of Travancore are miniature reproductions of churches in Portugal. With their whitewashed façades turned towards the sea, they seem to typify an incurable nostalgia for the land where their style of architecture more truly belongs. This tendency to feel a permanent debt to Europe and to imitate her ways and her customs has remained a dominant trait in all Goanese Christians, and this fact may explain why so many inhabitants of Goa seem unable to feel that they are true citizens of India.

Fortunately for the native inhabitants, the southern temperament of the Portuguese was not too sharply opposed to the mentality and feelings of the Indians. Just as the imported Baroque architecture mysteriously harmonized with the tropical landscape, so did the Portuguese bring natural sympathy and understanding to the task of developing the minds of the natives. The didactic rationalism and dry catholicism of the later missionaries was quite alien to them.

They knew how to make the principles of their faith attractive by combining them with the festivities and ritual so dear to the hearts of the pageantry-loving Indians. It has been said that the conversion of Goa was achieved through the pomp of Roman Catholic observances. The impressive ceremonial of mass baptisms, which was accompanied by mystery plays, dances and processions, was a great assistance to Christian propaganda and, in the eyes of simple people, seemed to prove the truth of the new religion. At all events the missionaries succeeded in showing that in addition to insisting on her fundamental principles and dogma the Church also knew how to give expression to the shining joy and inward happiness which exists in every human heart.

The Church calendar, rich in festival days, was used as a constant reminder to the population of the great truths of their new faith, and of the chief events of religious history as recorded in the Gospels—the Nativity, the Resurrection, the Ascension of Christ, Pentecost and the Coming of the Holy Ghost.

In many of the Christian communities established in those days, these old festival traditions are still alive. There is, for instance, the performance of the Passion Play, beginning on Palm Sunday with the entrance of Our Lord into Jerusalem, and reaching its climax on Good Friday with the Way of the Cross. In Dindigul, the stage is still set for these Passion Plays whose dialogue has come down by word of mouth. The meeting of Christ, carrying the Cross, with His Mother, is presented in chanted speeches of great pathos, which last for almost an hour. Some people of a Puritan outlook are deeply shocked by these Goanese religious festivities. But actually they are a unique mixture of European liturgical ceremonial and South Indian custom—a combination in which are mingled burning devotion and frolicsome gaiety, the sweet scent of incense, and the sulphurous smell of rockets; the chanting of the choir and the sound of gunfire; the light of wax candles and the glimmer of Chinese lanterns; stately processions and merry-go-rounds—a cross between a religious ceremony and a fair. Yet these surprising manifestations may well indicate that the ancient missionaries were, in spite of their European outlook, nearer in spirit to the native population than we are sometimes prone to believe; and that the Indian Christians themselves found a way to adapt the religion from the West to their own habits and beliefs. Thus the Goanese Church not only looks to the West for teaching and inspiration, but has finally evolved a completely original manner of worship, suitable to the traditions of the country.

One is therefore inclined to wonder whether modern critics, in spite of their extensive theological learning, are right to cast doubt on the soundness of Portuguese missionary methods. Naturally, it would be unwise to set much store by the religious value of the first mass conversions; but it is undeniable that the Christian faith strengthened and expanded with the second generation of converts who became the true heirs of the missionary saints. Throughout the eighteenth and nineteenth centuries the Christians of Daman, Cochin and Mylapore succeeded in preserving their faith intact, in spite of the fact that they suffered a grave lack of spiritual direction. They even increased impressively in numbers, for their company grew by some million souls.

During the last hundred years members of the Indian Roman Catholic Church have travelled widely in search of new opportunities for secular employment, journeying into the interior of India, and overseas even as far as East Africa. They may be found in many places, sometimes as members of the labouring classes, and also among the small groups of Indian middle-class families, while occasionally Christian Indians are members of the learned professions or hold office in Government service. Any Catholic priest who travels by rail in India, or visits the large towns, is sure of finding genuine support from members of these far-flung groups. He will encounter in such families men of unbreakable faith, full of the desire to assist fellow-Christians; sincerely devout women, and young people determined to live up to the highest ideals.

The Europeanized outlook of the Goanese—for which they cannot be blamed—has contributed to the regrettable misunderstanding caused by the belief that Roman Catholicism is a purely European religion, organized by, and dependent on, alien colonial power; and in the last resort incompatible with Indian national culture. The exceptionally authoritative attitude which the original churches founded by the Portuguese adopted after the seventeenth century led to administrative difficulties, and clashes within the organization, which seriously hindered the development of the Church in India. The wording of Papal Bulls showed that the supremacy of the Kings of Portugal was to extend to all lands discovered by the Portuguese, thus unambiguously the whole of India; and this supremacy carried with it the strict duty of bringing true religion to the country, and organizing the Church. Actually, Portuguese control never extended beyond the narrow coastal strip, and in the course of time the remarkable power of that comparatively small nation weakened, and the unique position which Portugal formerly held was won successively by the Dutch and by the British.

Only sporadic attempts at conversion were made in the vast, almost endless plains of the north, and in the highlands of the Deccan, which were then ruled by Mohammedan princes; and as time went on this state of affairs could not satisfy the ambitions of the Church of Rome.

In 1622 Pope Gregory XIII created within the framework of the Roman Catholic missionary council a central authority with full plenary powers; and he attempted through this to force Lisbon to agree that missionaries from the Vatican should undertake the campaign of spreading the Gospel in India. Conflict was now unavoidable. The more Portugal felt her political power to be slipping from her, the more desperately did she cling to her ecclesiastical authority. In doing this she was theoretically in the right. But her action was ill-judged, and in fact by insisting on her original privileges she damaged the higher interests of the Catholic Church. Lisbon could not prevent her supremacy being gradually undermined during the nineteenth century; and indeed the British Empire eventually assumed the position of preponderant power once held by the Church of Rome in India. Today we can hardly imagine the bitterness which this shrinkage of power caused at the time. In Madras, Calcutta and above all in Bombay, where the Goanese influence had been predominant, the struggle for power, with mutual accusations and even insults, nearly brought the Catholic communities to the brink of destruction. Violence resulted when it came to the actual possession of the churches. On these ecclesiastical battlefields, the spectacle of two warring Christian Churches facing each other in stubborn opposition was indeed a melancholy one. Distressing though these events were, it must be borne in mind that they had their origin in the fact that the Goanese priesthood felt that their deepest loyalty was to the Mother Church in Portugal. Owing to these complicated events, which caused the Vatican to withdraw some of the privileges originally granted—perhaps with undue haste—to the Indian Catholic Church, the last vestiges of Goanese influence in the Indian Union have disappeared. The ecclesiastical rights of the Patriarch of Goa are now limited to the territory that still belongs to Portugal.

But the position which the old Church of Goa was forced to relinquish is now beginning to be regained; and she is building on a better foundation through the younger generation of her members. Peace and quiet having returned to the community, the true spirit of religion has been reborn. Many of the sons of the Christian Goanese families have heard the call to the religious life, and have entered the priesthood or joined one of the monastic orders; and it has now become possible for the missionaries to hand over one diocese after the other to the care of the Indian priests, while a growing number of bishoprics are now occupied by Indian prelates, most of whom are the sons of families resident in the original Portuguese religious settlements. So after long years of unhappiness the Indian Church which had suffered from divisions and misunderstandings has, at last, taken her true place in the Christian fold, and become a Church of hope, which is thriving in the new free climate of India. It is therefore easy to understand that in these Catholic circles there is a deep and ever-stronger wish to see their homeland of Goa united with the great motherland of India by a free and spontaneous gesture.

Those, however, who appreciate the strength of the long-established links which bind Portugal to the last of her Indian possessions can easily understand why she will not easily be persuaded to relinquish Goa. In any case such a decision could not be lightly undertaken. Long association and tradition have stamped this part of the Indian peninsula with an indelible impression. Goa differs sharply in both its administrative and cultural development from the rest of the sub-continent. Apart from economic advantages which the people may derive from the present political situation, the 400,000 Roman Catholic inhabitants of Goa rejoice in a religious heritage which they cannot—nor would they ever desire—to relinquish. They would have to be absolutely certain that their religious rights would be safeguarded before they could agree to any sort of union with the Indian Republic, which, however much it may claim to be completely neutral from a religious point of view, is still inhabited by an overwhelming majority of devout Hindus, whose spirit exercises a certain domination over the activities of the State. Whatever the future of Goa may prove to be, let us hope that the lot of this predominantly Catholic land, with its highly individual culture, will be finally settled by peaceful means, and in accordance with the free choice of its inhabitants.

28. *St Francis Xavier with a Portuguese caravel and a sloop (a silver plaque with a relief from his shrine at Goa)*

29. *Death of St Francis Xavier in Sanzian in 1552 (a silver plaque with a relief from his shrine at Goa). Indian work after a European engraving, 1637*

30. *Potters carrying their goods to market*

31. *Pottery market at Goa*

32. *Ruined church near Poonakayal, probably built by the Dutch*

33. *Pre-Portuguese (?) Cross, near Cape Comorin, known as 'St Thomas's Cross'*

34. *Consecration of the church in Margao, Goa*

35. *Inner court of a deserted convent in Old Goa*

36. *Statues of saints on a stand in the open-air market at Margao*

37. *Woman wearing the Portuguese* velho *or veil, entering the church in Navelim near Goa*

38. *Indian Christian praying*

39. *Altar of St Ignatius of Loyola in the Jesuit Church in Old Goa*

28

29

30

31

32

33

34

35

36

37

IHS

In the Highlands of the Deccan

THE road which we took from Goa to the thickly wooded slopes of the Ghats and then on to the highlands of the Deccan was narrow, but still practical for motors. Near the coast the view is shut in by palm forests, but once the dry plateau of the Deccan has been reached, the eye commands vast stretches of shallow valleys and gently sloping hills. Here and there a flat-topped mountain, like a truncated cone, raises its steep bastions from the expanse of the surrounding plain, which gradually slopes from the peaks of the western Ghats towards the eastern shores. This point marks the water-shed. Hundreds of rivulets rise from the rain-drenched mountain ranges, and flowing down their sides, unite to form mighty rivers—the Godaveri, the Kistna, the Cauvery and others. Violent basaltic lava eruptions during the latter part of the Cretaceous period and possibly at the beginning of the Eocene period of the earth's history are responsible for the disastrously poor soil in the valleys and slopes of the Deccan trap area. During the dry season it is seamed with deep cracks and fissures, but with the coming of the June monsoons, rain once more softens the earth, which retains the welcome humidity for a very considerable time. The ground having thus become suddenly fertile, a variety of crops can be produced, including several kinds of millet, wheat, cotton and also the recently introduced sugar cane.

Although the Deccan is part of the state of Bombay, it is mostly inhabited by Mahrattas. This hardy and abstemious race of peasants only made their appearance in history during the seventeenth century. Under the leadership of their national hero, the bold and unlucky Shivaji, they rebelled against their Mohammedan overlords, the great Moghuls of Delhi. In the following century Mahratta princes conquered vast tracts of land in Central India and founded ruling dynasties including that of the Gaekwar of Baroda. Mean-time in Poona, their capital, the Peshwa or Chief Minister, a member of the brilliantly endowed Chitpāwan Brahmins, had seized the reins of power, and it was not before 1802 that the British succeeded in subjugating the warlike Mahrattas. Indeed, Poona has always remained a stronghold of Indian nationalism. It produced pioneers of the independence movement, leaders like Tilak and Ghokale who were among the founders of the Congress Party; and opened the way for Gandhi. Nor does it seem to be by mere

40. Mahratta water-carriers in Sangamner

chance that the Mahatma fell a victim to an attack by a fanatical Brahmin from Poona, for his tolerance of the Mohammedans had roused the hatred of the Hindu nationalists.

In Mahārāshtra, as the Mahrattas call their country, the Hindu religion still remains unchallenged. On the roads of the Deccan we constantly met pilgrims on their way to Nasik, or Pandharpur. The memory of their religious chants and of those who first performed them—such as the singers Dnyaneshwar, Namdev and Eknath—remain vividly alive in the minds of the people. They all hold fast to the true Bhakti doctrine, which aims at absolute union with the Deity (Krishna) through complete submission of the heart. These devout seekers after God have written many impressive hymns which well deserve to be placed, together with the Bhagavad Gita, as among the most precious of the Indian religious writings. Here is a free translation of a 'psalm' by Namdev who lived in Pandharpur during the thirteenth century:

> Whether I live or die
> My heart relies on Pandurang (God).
> Never shall I stop kneeling at your feet.
> I swear it by your name, Pandharinath.
> May his blessed name be for ever on my lips
> And in my heart everlasting love.

And Namdev spake:

> "O my God, help me to continue in such a way."

The most popular poet of the Mahrattas, however, is Tukaram, who was born at Dehu, near Poona, in 1608. Sometimes in his poems he appears to hold the belief in one god, whereas earlier psalm-writers remain firm in their pantheistic beliefs. Tukaram wrote:

> Thou, O my God, art my Mother, my Father, all my Love and
> Possessions.
> Thou art my everything. Thou it is who worketh my Salvation
> O God.
> Listen to my words, Pandurang,
> For I have become Thy servant and Thy slave.
> Save me, according to Thy Ways,
> For I stand lonely and lost in front of the dark future.

In the evenings the Mahrattas will listen for hour after hour to singers chanting these so-called *bajans*, or other religious songs. Alas, however, the official religion of these people does not seem to inspire sincere belief and piety in spite of the fact that temples tower high above the houses which nestle round them in villages and towns all over Mahārāshtra. Situated in such an arid countryside, inhabited by so lean and poor a race, the temples naturally do not display the overwhelming wealth of those in Southern India. Nor do the temples of Nasik enjoy the popularity or draw so large a number of worshippers as those of Madurai or Tiruchirapally. At all events the Bombay administration has found itself compelled to place the property of the temples, and their adjoining religious institutions (which often possess considerable wealth), under Government control. So far as can be observed on the banks of the holy Godaveri river near Nasik, the worship which the local inhabitants accord to their gods seems to consist solely in the performance of magical rites. It is highly distressing to see with what intent faces the devout follow the intricate ceremonies unfolded in the temples, while a Brahmin priest mumbles with apparent indifference, the liturgical prayers or the instructions which it is his duty to recite. It would be difficult to recognize the inspired spirit of a Tukaram among the countless sullen-faced Sadhus who, in Nasik and various other places, display their self-inflicted tortures to the amazed and gaping crowds.

Yet in spite of such repellent or superstitious practices, and however much the simple faith of the people has been misled, it would be very rash, and indeed wrong, to judge the faith of the Indian peoples by such superficial observations. In India, as elsewhere, genuine religious devotion avoids any indiscreet publicity, and beneath the strange forms of worship which I have described will be found a deep and honest desire to find eternal truth.

41. *Evening on the Kistna river in South Mahārāshtra*

42. *Herd of cattle grazing in the Deccan*

43. *Pilgrim on the way to Pandharpur*

44. *Hindus celebrating the* Pongul *(New Year) by attending a temple service*

45. *Statues of gods guarding the entrance to the 'Hall of the Thousand Columns'*

46. *Secular occupation in a temple*

47. *Magical sacrificial rites being performed in Nasik*

48. Sadhu *(penitent) in Nasik*

49. *Sacred cows wandering through the market place at Nasik*

50. *Shakuntala*

51. *Pariah women carrying earth for the construction of a dam near Nasik*

Phoenix

48

49

52

53

A Mission to the Pariahs in Mahārāshtra

WHILE staying in a small town during our drive through the Deccan, we heard our host casually refer to a Brahmin's daughter whose talent as a dancer was said to be unsurpassed. We asked him to try and get permission from the graceful Shakuntala to photograph her performance. Negotiations, which were carried on through various intermediaries, lasted for two long days, after which the young dancer consented, by permission of her father, to dance for us. A lofty roof terrace, part of the house of an equally high-born Brahmin —which could not be overlooked by an inquisitive neighbour—was chosen as the meeting-place. Shakuntala appeared, accompanied by her married sister, danced silently to the music of an Indian film song, 'Poem and Joy of Love', and then disappeared without having exchanged one word with us foreigners. We felt a deep admiration for a nation which knows how to value and to shelter its dearest jewels with such tender care. Experiences of this kind teach one to beware of hasty judgments about foreign customs and morals, or to criticize rashly the much-maligned caste-system of the Hindus. The rules and prescriptions of this system provide Hindu society with the counterpart of our Christian moral code by maintaining order, and protecting the official status, and the personal dignity of woman.

Yet the rules of the caste-system were undoubtedly the source of far-reaching evils, for, as their grip on society stiffened, they became deadly weapons in the hands of a selfish, aristocratic oligarchy and, finally, resulted in the condemnation of millions of people to a fate worse than slavery. In Mahārāshtra, as in every other part of India, unlucky Pariahs or Untouchables exist whose hopeless condition cries out to high heaven for justice. The Indian Parliament has only quite recently abolished the caste-system and insisted that no discrimination whatsoever should be made between the different classes of citizen, while heavy penalties have been instituted for those who trespass against these new edicts. Before the Members of Parliament unanimously took this all-important decision, the Minister for Home Affairs, Pandit Pant, entreated them to "banish and throw out of this country the devil of Untouchability". These words must recall to everyone the acts of Christ in driving out devils, as recorded in the Holy Gospels.

Indeed, one might almost say that the abolition of Untouchability is a

52. Starving Pariah children

53. Pariah mother outside her miserable mud hut

victory for Christian thought and, perhaps, an unwanted recognition by the dominant class of Hindus of the power of Christian missionaries. Gandhi's example undoubtedly had a decisive influence on bringing about this reform, but, then, did not Gandhi himself admit that he had been inspired on the subject by the Sermon on the Mount?

He was also fully aware of the good work done by thousands of Catholic and Protestant missionaries among the Pariahs. For the third, and most modern era of evangelization in India, which started gradually, after the effect of the turmoils and new ideals of the French Revolution had been digested, directed its most intensive effort towards the conversion of the lowest, caste-less strata of the population of India.

Our journey through the land of the Mahrattas gave us the opportunity of becoming better acquainted with the so-called missionaries to the Pariahs, who, as compatriots, offered us the most friendly hospitality. Since 1854 Swiss and German Jesuits have been active in Poona and in the adjoining more northerly districts of the state of Bombay. They started by gathering together into organized parishes those Roman Catholics who had moved into their district from Goa and regions farther south, and later in the eighteen-seventies they began to extend to the Mahars the work of preaching the Gospel. These people, who were the original inhabitants of the country, appear to have been reduced by the invading Mahrattas to a sort of bodily slavery, and then branded as Pariahs. Each village has its well-separated and clearly defined 'Mahar-wada' or Mahar quarter. Here the landless slaves live in miserable mud huts. Previously they were serfs attached to the soil, without the right to change their dwelling-place. They carried out the lowest duties for the other villagers, yet they were not allowed to draw water at the communal well, nor to enter any *kumbi*-house. The worst features of this degrading custom were abolished under the British Raj, yet the actual situation of the Mahars was very little bettered. With selfless dedication and unlimited patience the missionaries slowly and gradually began to improve the condition of these unfortunate people by building a number of dispensaries and homes for the sick, founding schools, feeding the hungry in times of famine, and thus, little by little, they succeeded in raising the position of the Christian Pariahs.

54. *Student washing an Untouchable child*

55. *Huts for the accommodation of temporary workers at the sugar factory of Belapur*

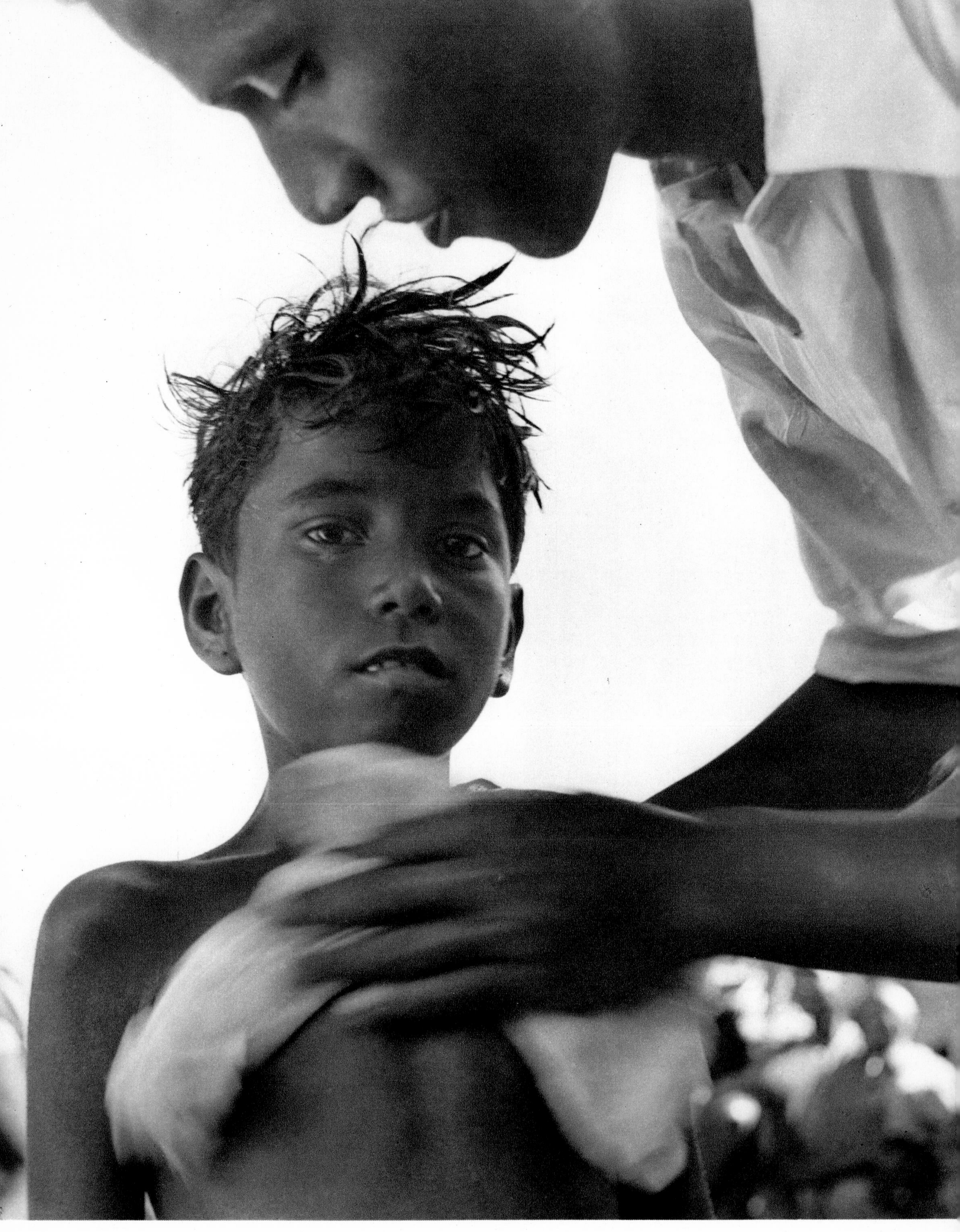

This social rehabilitation and practical help was, however, never used to bribe the Pariahs into taking an interest in Christianity. But it proved—and continues to prove—an invaluable method of helping a despised group of people to regain the self-respect and self-confidence of which they had been completely robbed, and to draw them out of the fatalistic mental twilight in which they existed. A certain amount of human dignity is a necessary quality before any human being can gain an understanding of the social and spiritual responsibilities which a good Christian must bear. Today the German-Swiss Jesuit Mission counts some 20,000 Christian Mahars among its members.

Yet the priests frankly admitted that they are not yet entirely satisfied with the spiritual development of some of their converts. There is much still to be desired, especially in those distant villages which priests can visit but rarely. On the whole, however, the progress made is striking. Today the *kumbis* or peasants are actually envious of the Mahars because they have the chance of sending their children to well-organized schools. The parents today are also beginning to realize the value of the education given to their daughters by the nuns, who undertake the upbringing of the girls. The Christian workers in the sugar factories have resisted the blandishments of local Communist agents, and so have those who have sought work in the towns where higher pay is obtainable. A number of native teachers and catechumens have developed into faithful and gifted colleagues, who during the course of the well-attended religious ceremonies know how to express the Christian message in *bajans* of their own composition. A few years ago the Mahars themselves formulated a request for the founding of a high school for their benefit, and today the best of its pupils study in Sangamner, seated on the same school benches as the sons of the Brahmins, and even have their meals with them in the Scouts' Camps which they now attend. Indeed, there have been many changes in Mahārāshtra since 1870.

Our account of the Jesuit Mahar Missions is equally applicable to the work done by the Capuchins for the Untouchable Chamars in the Ganges plateau, and to the activities of many other missions belonging to various nationalities whose care is bestowed on the Mahars of the east coast and in other districts.

56. *Woman weaving in Sangamner*

57. *Nun teaching a Pariah widow to operate a knitting machine*

The influence of Christian missionaries on the Pariahs, of whom India has some forty millions, produced such remarkable results that even the non-Christian Untouchables began to put forward claims for the improvement of their social position. During the nineteen-thirties this movement to achieve freedom, which was initiated by Dr Ambedkar, a highly educated Mahar, assumed such importance that the Hindu leaders realized that they must make some concessions. They wished at all costs to avoid the threatened mass-conversion of Pariahs to an alien faith, and thus they tried to ensure a continued general adherence to the native religion by slowly and gradually opening the doors of the temples to the Untouchables. They also approved that article of the Indian Constitution, itself decisively influenced by Dr Ambedkar, as the first Minister of Justice in free India, affirming the equality before the law of the Untouchables. The first step taken by Nehru's government was to go into the question of providing relief for "India's millions of suffering sons", a company which, of course, includes the Pariahs; and after careful thought measures were taken to improve their lot. Thus the spirit of the Sermon on the Mount and that of true Christian love which are faithfully practised and preached by missionaries of all Christian denominations have brought about a social revolution which is changing the face of modern India, and has forced Hinduism itself to reform its social institutions.

In Shiva's Holy City

In Shiva's Holy City, *Tiru Shiva Pali* (today spelt alternatively Tiruchirapally or Trichinopoly), we were able to study yet another typical aspect of modern Christian India. As the main efforts of the nineteenth- and twentieth-century missionaries were concentrated on the conversion of the Pariahs, it is only natural that they should have achieved their most striking successes in this field; yet this did not prevent them from obtaining equally remarkable results among Hindus and Mohammedans through the medium of their excellent intermediary and high schools. On the Roman Catholic side it was the Jesuits who, in accordance with their traditions, concentrated their chief activities on education. Working in the vast field assigned to them, an area which extended over the provinces of Bombay, Bengal and Madras, the University Colleges which they founded in each of these states are among the most important in India.

St Joseph's College in Tiruchirapally, that famous stronghold of South Indian Brahminism, is one of the oldest and best known of these colleges. Here the Jesuits revived, on modern lines, the work of a predecessor of genius, Father Robert de Nobili, who began his mission in near-by Madurai during the seventeenth century. This was the period of 'Europeanization' in Goa, where the Portuguese missionary methods, as described in an earlier chapter, achieved lasting results, partly because the new converts were completely severed from their former Hindu background. The reaction of the Brahmins to this independent behaviour was deeply to despise the Christians, who, in their eyes, were traitors to India's traditional culture and had inflicted deep wounds on the caste-system. The Goanese Christian, like the Portuguese themselves, was contemptuously referred to as *Frangi* (Frank—term used in the East to describe a European). He lost caste, sank lower than a Pariah, and was outlawed as a man with whom the orthodox Hindu could not associate. The inexorability of such autocratic social rules can hardly be conceived by a modern European, yet they still hold good in India, and are one of the greatest drawbacks to the conversion of members of the higher castes. The degree of aversion for everything Christian which still reigns in certain Hindu circles is clearly illustrated by the wording on the notices which I myself saw at the entrance of certain temples. It read, "Pariahs, dogs and Europeans are strictly forbidden to enter".

The spread of the Christian faith in the interior of India was only possible if the missionaries were willing to pay tribute in a large measure to the customs of the country and to make an effort to allow the highly born converts still to conform to the rules and prescriptions of their caste, so long as these did not conflict with the teachings of the Church. Father de Nobili was the initiator of this new form of evangelization. He came to Madurai, then the spiritual centre of South Indian Brahminism, in 1606. He adopted the clothing and the bearing of a *Sanyasi* (penitent) and, having carefully studied the religious literature of the Hindus, he tried to adapt their method of reasoning to his own purpose. He actually believed that it might be possible to prove that the prevailing Hindu religion, with its multiplicity of gods and magic ritualism, stood in complete contradiction to the pure teachings of the Vedas. He also held, probably with reason, that the caste-system had originally started as a lay prerogative of the upper classes, and had only later been incorporated into the religious framework. He thus allowed the high-caste converts to observe their rules where food, bathing, behaviour to the Pariahs and such customs were concerned. Other practices became Christianized—as, for instance, the wearing of a religious caste-sign on the forehead, which was replaced by a symbolic cross.

De Nobili and his Jesuit followers, known as *Panguswamys*, obtained important results. About 1750 the Madurai Mission could boast of some 200,000 Christians. This large and important community enjoyed Indian citizenship because it did not come into conflict with the customs of the country, and included members of all castes among its converts. The mission also succeeded in weathering the catastrophes which overtook it after 1750 as the result of events which had occurred in Europe—the expulsion from several countries and temporary suppression of the Order of Jesus, the failure of longed-for new missionaries to arrive in the field, and jurisdictional differences between the Vatican's Congregation for Propaganda and the Portuguese Church leaders.

When in 1837 the French Jesuits took over the largest part of the old Madurai Mission, their methods of evangelization had to be adapted to changing times. But the original aim of bringing high-caste Hindus into the Christian fold remained the same. The answer to this problem was sought by the establishment of high schools. In 1835 Macaulay had published his minute on the educational system which should be adopted in India. The question was whether the rising generation of Indians was to be given a culture based on an Oriental pattern, or one copied from Western methods. He inclined to the second answer in agreement with the opinions of the Indian intelligentsia of

58. Christian Mahar widows singing hymns at the Poona Mission station

the day, under the leadership of Ram Mohan Roy. Consequently a number of high schools (the equivalent of the Swiss *Mittelschulen* or intermediary schools) were established. The year 1857 saw the foundation of the universities of Bombay, Calcutta and Madras, which during the course of the century were followed by several others. Run on the English model, they were "corporations aiming at the passing of examinations", giving the students guidance in the technique of teaching and granting to the successful candidates certificates in place of academic degrees.

General education was given in schools, run, as in England, by private individuals or by corporate bodies. No one was excluded from attending or from receiving financial aid, as the British Government made a point of remaining strictly non-denominational. The Protestant missions, however, which now began a powerful drive, brought their greatest efforts to bear in the educational field, and this example was followed by the Roman Catholics as soon as their strength and their means allowed them to do so. In due course the Hindus and the Mohammedans gradually began to create educational centres, and finally the Indian State has opened its own colleges. Today the new Indian universities tend to model themselves on those of the European continent.

We must now return to Shiva's Holy City. Here the great temple, set on its famous rock, dominates the uneven sea of houses. At its feet, and in the immediate vicinity of the Brahmins' residential quarter, stands St Joseph's College. This consists of a large compound containing school buildings, laboratories, students' quarters, a church and a monastery, and playing-fields. Founded at Negapatam in 1844, the university was transferred to its present site in 1883. Father de Nobili's dream has been fulfilled; a Christian school now stands in the very heart of a stronghold of Hindu Brahminism.

Many contacts and much friendship have been established between the Catholic priests and the 'Sons of the Gods' (or Brahmins). Today there are some 1,500 pupils at St Joseph's and about 1,900 university students. Of

59. Tatia-Master, a remarkable catechumen, Sangamner

60. Pupils studying in the courtyard of the Jesuit school at Sangamner in the cool of the evening

61. In the St François de Sales Technical School, Madras

this total, about 1,300 are Christians and the remainder are Hindus, mostly of the Brahmin caste. In addition to the twenty Jesuit priests who run the schools there are forty-five teachers and seventy-one professors, who include a large percentage of Hindus. Pupils can study philology, history, economics, mathematics, physics, and there are chemical laboratories and a practical engineering section.

The scientific level of an Indian high school cannot be compared with that of a European university. Colleges in the sub-continent are more concerned with teaching than with research and only too many students merely set out to master the subjects required to pass examinations without developing any genuine scientific interests. Those who wish to find posts in the rapidly expanding Indian industrial concerns or in the newly established Government Research Institutions must go abroad to complete their higher studies.

St. Joseph's College has produced thousands of graduates, a great number of whom have entered politics, taken administrative posts or gone in for agriculture. Several have served their country in the highest government positions. These old boys are indeed to be found everywhere. A majority preserve for their *Alma Mater*, and the Roman Catholic priests who taught them, a deep affection and respect, but no feeling of moral dependence. It is a curious experience, when visiting the near-by temple of Srirangam, to meet orthodox Brahmins who in the course of conversation refer to the fact that they are former pupils of the Jesuits. Such remarks go to prove that, however much the missionaries' ultimate aim is to convert their pupils, they strive to maintain in their schools an honourable respect for the religious beliefs of their students. This consideration is so great that in the boarding schools, as opposed to the day schools, three different dining-rooms are arranged—one for Christians, the second for Hindus in general, and the third for vegetarian Hindus.

On the other hand, the tuition given to the boys tries to free them from any surviving prejudices of the caste-system. We accompanied a group of students, Christians and Hindus, to a Pariah settlement which they visit regularly as social workers. The young men called the children together, washed the little Untouchables with their own hands, oiled their black mops of hair, fed them and then cleaned the narrow streets between the

62. Chemistry laboratory, St Joseph's College, Tiruchirapally

63. View of part of the College

62

63

64

65

miserable huts, mended the straw roofs and so on. To perform such menial tasks in India amounts to a social revolution, yet they were carried out by choice and with goodwill by the pick of St Joseph's students. Conversions to Christianity are, by contrast, extremely rare. There have been, it is true, some remarkable exceptions, for actually in Tiruchirapally a few Brahmins have found their way into the Catholic Church, in spite of the strong opposition of their families. Several of these converts have taken their vows as members of the Society of Jesus.

Everything we have said about the Tiruchirapally College is equally true of the other Roman Catholic university colleges in India—the St Xavier College in Bombay, a foundation of the Swiss Jesuit missionary Father P. Willi; the Loyola College in Madras; and the educational institutions in Calcutta, Patna and so forth. During 1952, the Roman Catholic Church maintained nineteen of these first-class colleges, attended by some 20,000 students, as well as a number of specialized schools and also 250 intermediary schools with about 150,000 pupils. As the Protestant educational organizations are about equally strong in numbers, it is clear that Christian missionaries have made an imposing contribution to the solution of India's burning educational problem.

From the missionary point of view it is possible to say that the high schools have succeeded in completing the levelling of class distinctions, and in consequence have raised the status and the spiritual condition of the Pariahs. In the past, missionaries in Goa had estranged the natives through their exaggerated Europeanism; apparently the modern missions have also created a prejudice in some Indian circles, namely that they are a 'Pariah Church'. This was a criticism which I heard only too often, especially in areas situated far from any sort of Christian high school. The better class Hindu may, then, be said to judge the missionaries as some educated men at home might judge the Salvation Army. They express admiration for the selflessness of these good people, but they would not dream of joining their ranks. Yet one of the fundamental duties of the missionary university colleges is to give the members of the Indian upper classes an opportunity to make contacts with Christians and to develop sympathy with the tenets of Christian behaviour.

64. *Jesuit and Brahmin, Tiruchirapally*

65. *Indian Government Chemical Research Institute, Poona*

66. *Girl students at the College of St Sophia, Bombay*

67. *Brahmin girls in the College of the Holy Cross, Tiruchirapally*

68. *Young mother in St Anne's Hospital, Vijayavada*

69. *Siesta hour in the Hospital*

70. *Ritual purification of a young Hindu mother at the Vijayavada Hospital*

71. *Native nun, Chota Nagpur*

66

67

68

69

Tiruchirapally to Vijayavada

DURING the trip our admiration was aroused again and again by the marvellous work of the Roman Catholic missionary sisters. At Tiruchirapally and two other of our 'ports of call' we were able to study the achievements of these valiant women under particularly striking and memorable conditions. Today it is impossible to think of Christian India without the presence and the active work of the Roman Catholic nuns, and one is inclined to wonder why they did not make their appearance in the missionary field before the nineteenth century. The explanation probably lies in the conditions of the past. At the time when the early missionaries began their work, masculine chivalry may well have caused men to hesitate to submit women to the hardships of the sea voyage and the discomfort, and even danger, to which evangelists were exposed.

Yet the essential reason lies elsewhere. It is to be found in the strict regulations, which ever since mediaeval times have ruled convents. There was only one form of life for members of women's religious orders—the rigorously cloistered existence for which they had left the world and pronounced their eternal vows. Not until the eighteenth century was the severity of Canon Law slightly relaxed in the case of a few newly established religious orders for women; and only during the nineteenth century did the idea of using the collaboration of nuns in missionary work in distant parts of the world come to be accepted. In the meantime the conditions of life in countries such as India had greatly improved owing to the administration of the British Government; and a constantly growing number of women, belonging to old-established and newly created religious orders, joined the men in their missionary work. Today they completely outnumber the men, and it is impossible to imagine a mission station without women. In the field of welfare and the education of girls the sisters have now taken the leading place.

They are responsible for the entire upbringing of the Christian Indian girls, beginning with the kindergarten, continuing in primary and upper schools, and on to the university colleges now open to women. Those who teach the most advanced subjects come more and more into contact with girls of the upper classes, whether Hindu or Mohammedan. In Tiruchirapally, for instance, we visited the girls' college, run by Sisters of the Cross, and found that of the 500 girls they taught, two-thirds belonged to Hindu families of high rank. One could hardly imagine a more delightful sight than this group of young women (many of the students are married) in their becoming *saris*, who, in spite of some shyness, impressed us with their friendly and natural manners. Their genuine respect and affection for the teachers produces complete confidence, and this often results in setting the nuns very difficult problems to solve. India's religious toleration extends to the acceptance of the co-existence of all creeds within its realm, but it does not go so far as to admit conversion of individuals to an alien faith.

According to the statistics of 1952, the Roman Catholic Sisters run twenty-one colleges, in which they teach some 6,000 pupils, whereas similar Protestant institutions undertake the education of about 4,000 girls.

When it comes to primary and intermediate schools the attendance figures reach some 200,000 girls in each category respectively. Similar types of boys' schools can claim about 500,000 pupils. These figures clearly indicate that girls hardly lag behind their brothers in their eagerness to study in Roman Catholic educational institutions. This is quite astonishing and it is a state of affairs that has greatly helped to improve the social position of Indian women, whose improved status is 'absolutely necessary', according to one of Nehru's statements in the Indian Parliament.

Welfare work and medical aid are also among the tasks undertaken by the sisters. Orphanages, homes for the aged, hospitals, dispensaries, leper settlements, infant welfare and nursing in the homes of the natives afford them endless opportunities to show their Christian love for all people, without discrimination of caste or religion; for misery is deep and widespread in India. The temptation is great to use charity and individual help as a means to obtain conversions, and to measure the success of the work according to the 'christening statistics'; and even the best of sisters may sometimes fall a victim to such a temptation.

Yet other missions do exhibit the spirit of Christian charity in all its purity. On our way towards the north we visited, in Madras, the Institute for the Blind and Deaf, run by Belgian nuns. It stands in the centre of a magnificent park, the value of whose beauty as a happy setting for the wards cannot be over-estimated. It is here that a number of India's four million blind children, and also several dozen deaf and dumb youngsters, are mothered and taught by the good sisters. Where would the Christian spirit be if the precious work performed and the efforts put forth here were expected by the

72. *In the Deaf and Dumb Institute of the Catholic nuns in Madras*

73. *Blind girl at her spinning wheel, Madras*

72

73

74

75

Church to bring practical results in the form of conversions? The nuns do good for the sake of goodness, because God is all good, and we must strive to resemble Him.

The selflessness and limitless Christian love displayed by the nuns in a country which has for centuries been rent asunder by caste prejudice is ample proof that the flower of the Christian Church has been called to carry on this work of charity and practical help. The name of Nehru and those of many other leading Indian personalities may be found in the visitors' book of the Institute. This shows that the quiet activity of the nuns has attracted the attention of the most influential people in the land, a gratifying and helpful tribute to the work of the Roman Catholic missions.

A long day's drive north of Madras brought us to Vijayavada, the new name for Bezwada, a busy town of moderate size, where the friendly welcome of the Sisters of St Anne from Lucerne helped us to forget the strain and fatigue induced by our hard and lengthy journey. These courageous women first came to India in 1927. Some of them took posts as nurses in a British Government hospital, and by dint of economizing on their wages, were able, within a few years, to set aside a sum sufficient—with the aid of a grant from the Mother House which doubled it—to enable them to start a small hospital of their own. Gifts from generous and grateful patients were responsible for enabling them to see a large modern building rise, stone by stone. In spite of some early disappointments—happily overcome today—with the medical staff, St Anne's Hospital has developed splendidly. Patients from near and far are brought to it in motor-cars, ox-carts, or even on stretchers, and the patients include a very large number of women suffering from serious complaints peculiar to their sex. Seventy-five per cent of the patients receive free treatment, and all of them are desperately poor.

Yet—it would seem almost by a miracle—the sisters always manage to overcome their financial difficulties. Some time ago the Mother Superior was awarded the Kaiser-i-Hind medal, which is given annually to one person in each province for special and meritorious social work. This is a rare,

74. *Folk-dance of the Oraon Brides, Chota Nagpur*

75. *Boys doing their early morning physical training in the school of Samtoli, Chota Nagpur*

much-prized and well-deserved recognition of the selfless devotion of an energetic woman and her assistant sisters.

St. Anne's is, also, one of the few hospitals owned by Roman Catholic missions, whereas the Protestants run over 350 hospitals, among which some are acknowledged as the best medical centres in India. This remarkable achievement commands our admiration, but, at the same time, it makes us wonder how and why this difference in numbers has occurred.

The answer is not as simple as it might seem. Financial difficulties may be partly responsible, but the real reason may well lie with certain Roman Catholic Church regulations which have been enforced until quite recently. For instance, Catholic nuns were forbidden to assist in maternity cases at the actual birth, and were also not supposed to receive their training as nurses in non-Catholic medical schools. These rules naturally meant that the Catholic sisters often lacked the first-rate medical training without which no modern hospital can be set up and efficiently run. Luckily, most of these disabilities have now been removed, especially as leading Catholic circles have realized that in modern missionary work high spiritual qualities are no longer sufficient, and that specialized qualifications and technical knowledge are indispensable. The example of the Sisters of St Anne at Vijayavada illustrates the results which a handful of skilled and competent women have been able to obtain.

Indian family life is going through a period of far-reaching change, in so far as woman has now 'come of age'. The reforms and prohibitions introduced by the British Government in India (laws against the burning of widows [*suttee*], child marriage and so forth) have been recognized by the Government of the Indian Republic. These regulations were reframed and enlarged before passing through the Indian Parliament in 1952. Indian women now enjoy the same rights as men, including that of suffrage; new marriage and inheritance laws have been instituted and much greater freedom has, in general, been granted to women to enter a number of occupations. The custom of Purdah, originally a Mohammedan rule which forbade women to appear in mixed assemblies, to take any part in public life, insisted on their being veiled and so on, has now been completely abandoned. The respect and consideration which Indian mothers have always enjoyed within the family circle is now being extended to the young bride, the married woman and the female citizen in general.

This improvement in women's condition and the evolution of the feminine ideal has developed, as Mrs Chandrakala Hate (a pioneer of the feminist movement in India since its inception) noted in her remarkable book, *The Indian Woman and Her Future*, in the face of considerable opposition from orthodox Hindus.

Yet these developments will only become lasting benefits to Indian society if the high moral values of the inherited culture can be carried over into the new way of life; above all, the unlimited protection given to the dignity of woman. After all, in spite of its repressive methods, the essential aim of the Purdah system was nothing else but the preservation of woman's purity. The greatest service these sisters can render, above and beyond their selfless works of charity and teaching, is to give Indian women the example of lives led in freedom and dignity.

Chota Nagpur—A Land without a Temple

THE huge triangular sub-continent of India is divided at the northern base by the chain of the Vindhya mountains, which separate the vast plains of the Indus and the Ganges rivers. Chota Nagpur lies at the point where the last easterly spurs of this wide mountainous range, with its many peaks and valleys, melt into the Bengal plain. Here important groups of the Indian aborigines or Adivasis still survive, protected by the primeval forests. Their matriarchal customs and their language seem to indicate that they belong to the Austro-Asiatic people who invaded these regions from the east and eventually intermarried with local Dravidian tribes. The main divisions are the Mundas, the Oraons and the Kharias, all of whom are listed as peoples holding the Animist creed. Chota Nagpur is a land without gods and without a temple. Situated in the very centre of Hindu India, it forms an island with a completely different culture and different beliefs.

In the seventeenth century the Adivasis, living in the isolation of their remote mountain country, found themselves threatened by Indian intruders. "A horde of people without scruples and lacking in charity descended on the entire region. The unlucky aborigines, who had once husbanded the soil and made it fruitful, saw themselves overwhelmed, robbed, oppressed and deprived of their precious acres because they had not in their innocence known how to protect themselves against the guile of the invaders." Some of the Indian rajahs established a kind of colonial rule over large tracts of this country, and the *zamindars* or tax collectors soon cunningly contrived, as they did elsewhere in India, to become landowners themselves. More and more of the peasants lost their fields, ever higher requisitions of crops were inflicted on them and more forced labour was continually demanded.

76. *Oraon farmstead*

77. *Missionary arriving in a Christian village, in Oraon*

78. *In accordance with traditional custom, the guest is received with a ceremonial washing of hands*

79. *Religious instruction in a village school*

80. *Missionary celebrating Mass and preaching in the courtyard of a school*

77

78

79

80

Moral degradation came in the wake of economic enslavement. Drunkenness spread and the whole population lapsed into generally brutish behaviour.

This was the situation when, some time in the eighteen-forties, German Lutheran missionaries first made contact with the Mundas and began to help them. But they made the mistake of overstepping their functions in encouraging their converts to seek political freedom. This brought them into conflict with the British administration and was, in fact, the cause of their losing most of their influence. Some thirty years later Roman Catholic missionaries, who were already established in Ranchi, began an evangelistic penetration into Chota Nagpur. They were Belgian Jesuits, with headquarters in Calcutta. Their early efforts proved disappointing, but in 1885 the young Father Lievens appeared, and soon proved himself to be one of the most remarkable missionaries of modern times.

From the beginning Father Lievens made intelligent use of the advice he received from a sympathetic *Jemadar* or police chief, who gave him information about the habits and customs of the country. He also heard of the initial successes and later mistakes of the Lutheran missionaries. The basic plan he adopted was to make a firm stand for the social rights of the Adivasis, but only in the degree that they had formerly enjoyed these; and he scrupulously avoided coming into conflict with the authorities. The claims which the natives in their ignorance and fear of reprisals had not dared to put forward, he now presented. He carried these claims before the incorruptible British tribunals, and won lawsuit after lawsuit.

The only reward he asked from the natives was for them to listen to his Christian teaching, and he sometimes persuaded whole villages thus to hear the Word.

Success came almost too rapidly. The Oraons, who live in the west of the country, came in their thousands to hear Father Lievens preach. The inhabitants of entire valleys declared themselves willing to accept the protection of the missionaries. Lievens realized that his goal was the conversion of an entire people; and, encouraged by the example of his great forerunner and model, St Francis Xavier, he did not hesitate to baptize his new converts after a very short period of religious instruction. During 1888, he christened over 11,000 persons and produced 40,000 catechumens in 832 villages.

Two years later, however, the crisis which he had feared came about. The number of missionaries entering the field was not sufficient to keep pace with

81. Heathen Oraon

their ever-increasing duties. Father Lievens himself had to leave India, completely exhausted, and he died of tuberculosis at the age of thirty-seven. New Principals of the Order were put in charge of the Chota Nagpur Mission, and they criticized the way in which the work had been carried on as injudicious. The *zamindars*, anxious about the taxes, tried to undermine the Catholic influence, and even the authorities became uneasy, as they feared that a new uprising might take place. In spite of such setbacks, the movement towards Christianity was too well under way to be easily checked. It even spread from the British-administered areas into the states of Jaipur and Gangpur, although their respective rajahs persecuted the Christians in the true sense of the word, in their dominions. The Belgian Jesuits, however, summoning up all their forces, succeeded in consolidating their communities, and brought the number of converts from 62,000 in 1901 to 150,000 in 1910. Today they owe their enduring success to the extension of their educational activities, and hardly less to the social and charitable organization which was the initial aim of the pioneers of the Order.

The ardent Belgian, Father Lievens, found a worthy successor in the methodical German, Father Hoffmann. At his earnest request the Government of Bengal finally decided in 1908 to pass the so-called Chota Nagpur Tenancy Act. By the terms of this Act 400 Munda villages were completely, and some 800 were partly, awarded the full and inalienable ownership of the land which had originally been theirs. Meanwhile Father Hoffmann had, in this country of primeval forests, established a Credit Bank and Co-operative Societies, both of which institutions have greatly helped the solution of agrarian problems all over India. The aim of the Bank was to provide cheap credit for definite agricultural enterprises to the peasants of Chota Nagpur, who until then had been the victims of usurers to whom they had to pay up to 75 per cent interest on loans.

Before a loan from the Bank can be obtained the Panchayat, or Council of Village Elders, must consider the demand which is presented by one of its members. If they pass it as justified, the request is forwarded to one of the branches of the Bank or to the central office in Ranchi. The village community must offer a certain guarantee for each loan in order that the Bank may be assured that interest will be paid and the conditions of the loan fulfilled. In 1934 the Bank had some 14,000 accounts from about 1,500 villages, and had a capital of several millions of rupees. The Bank, whose earnings must, in accordance with a statute, be divided among the shareholders, works hand-in-hand with a Buyers' Co-operative, and the so-called 'Rice Bank', which advances rice-seed to the peasants. After the harvest this is paid back in kind.

Apart from their administrative and evangelization work, the missionaries devoted much time and great efforts to educate the young Adivasis men. They systematically built schools and organized the teaching. At the same time various Orders of nuns undertook work for the welfare of the women. Domestic training schools were founded and the teaching of handicrafts instituted. Some of the best 'Brussels lace' is today made in Chota Nagpur. The ruinous marriage festivities, which are a financial burden on families all over India, were done away with once and for all. In every mission station the sisters bring all the girls of marriageable age together and instruct them in their 'Brides' School'. Then, on a carefully chosen day a large collective wedding is celebrated with great splendour, and at comparatively little cost to the families of the young couples, who now share the expense, instead of each one of them separately having to feed the whole village; and thus, as a result, falling heavily into debt.

Chota Nagpur now has 300,000 Adivasis Roman Catholics, together with a large number of Anglicans and members of other Protestant denominations. In the capital, Ranchi, the Roman Catholics possess a university college and a priests' seminary. Since 1951, this important diocese has been under the direction of Monseigneur Kujur, a Jesuit of Oraon birth. In 1947 I visited the modest mud hut in which he was born, and where his unassuming mother still lives. It stands in a small hamlet near Rengarth, where the few open fields are entirely surrounded by jungle in which tigers may still be found. This shows how the Jesuit mission, in a few short decades, has established a national Church with a spiritual life of its own. The outstanding social help which the Adivasis received from the Jesuits produced the necessary conditions for a reformation of their customs and morals; the inspiration which this ancient and yet vigorous people found in the Christian faith enabled them to achieve this 'renaissance'.

No one who has had the time and the courage to leave the well-trodden paths of the tourist in order to penetrate the so-called wilderness of Chota Nagpur, is likely to be able to resist the charm of its Christian aborigine population. Their farmsteads are so clean, their young men seem so gay, whether at work, at play or indulging in any sport; and they are indeed a happy people who know how to enjoy all festival days, and who show their piety by prayer and song during the well-attended ceremonies of their church.

Very recently the Government of the Madhya Pradesh (formerly the Central Provinces) thought it necessary to set up a commission to report on the 'missionary activities' in the region, the rumour having been spread by ill-natured critics that illegal methods had been used to force Adivasis to become 'converted'. When the commission reached a remote little market town called Gholeng, its leader expressed his unmitigated astonishment as follows: "We expected to encounter a half-savage jungle population here, and what did we find? A large and well-organized gathering of Adivasis, who expressed their views with dignity and in most convincing style. Among them were men with academic degrees, and other well-educated people, and girls who work as teachers even in our capital, Delhi." On their return several members of the commission made highly complimentary reports on what they had seen during their visit. "On the whole the Christian missionaries of Chota Nagpur have achieved remarkable results in both the educational and the medical fields" was their conclusion.

82. Oraon boy

83. Festival in the evening

84. Out of darkness into light

Bombay—Gateway to the West

THE Roman Catholic Church has today spread over the whole of India the network of her seventy dioceses and her many parishes. During our journey the information we gathered has convinced us that she not only exercises a well co-ordinated influence through the country, but also that she can, from her store of inner spiritual riches, bring comfort to people in every social strata. She takes good care of the children, the sick and the needy; and she feels at home with the peasants whose wells, fields and herds are the subjects of her motherly solicitude. Through the pupils of her high schools, she has also gained a foothold in Government circles, and here she is careful to keep in step with the development of modern ideas.

The large cities of India, such as Bombay, are becoming more and more inclined to adopt Western ways of life. The characterless concrete houses which have sprung up in endless rows all along the bay of Kolaba might just as well be standing on the shore at Rio de Janeiro. The huge limousines which race along the tarred streets of Bombay are identical with those which drive down the avenues in New York; the modern Indian buys the same fashion goods in the shops on Hornby Road that he would find in London in Bond Street; and in most Bombay cinemas the films shown are Hollywood productions, which are evidently able to achieve a universal box-office appeal.

We are witnessing the rise of a highly paradoxical situation. The more the Eastern countries succeed in freeing themselves from the domination of the West, the more zealously do they strive to imitate the technical civilization of their former overlords, harness its methods, and adapt its ideology to the service of their own peoples. Thus the problems facing modern Europe are also those to be found in Asiatic countries. The spiritual disintegration of our old continent has, in a measure, affected the whole world. Everywhere Christianity is fighting against rationalism, materialism and atheism which have of late found their most consistent expression in Communism.

Christian India has to fight an increasingly fierce battle on two fronts. On the one hand, it must stand up against the old heathen Hindu creed; on the other, it must struggle against modern de-Christianized tendencies which threaten its own ranks. In the great cities of India one hears complaints about a certain slackening of true religion. In Travancore, Communism

85. Blessing a new well

appears to have taken hold of the more ignorant section of Christian workers, as has happened in Italy. It has even been said that the missionaries teach the Indian people to read in order to allow Communist pamphlets to enjoy a wider field of propaganda. The non-denominational spirit of the high schools has been criticized as nurturing a generation without religion, ready to accept the teaching of Communism; and there are a certain number of facts which would appear to justify some of these accusations.

In any case, the Church finds herself faced with difficult problems which she must take into account. The two most urgent are undoubtedly Indian nationalism and the spread of Communism. Both, although for quite different reasons, make it essential for the Church to put forth every effort to train a trustworthy body of native priests. The sympathetic attitude of the British Government of India towards the missionaries had misled many non-Christian Indians into thinking the missionaries agents and dependents of the British Raj. The only way to disprove this accusation was to reinforce the Catholic clergy by increasing the number of Indian-born priests and by striving, whenever possible, to choose bishops from among these native clergy. It was hoped that these measures would dispel any mistaken ideas about the political attitude of the Catholic missionaries, and later be of help in dealing with the new, free India. There was also the possibility that an Indian National Government might make difficulties over the entrance of fresh foreign missionaries into the country, as has indeed proved to be the case. Moreover, the example of what has happened in Communist China, where within a few years all foreign missionaries have, almost without exception, been expelled or arrested, served as a warning, and convinced Rome that the only way to avoid a similar catastrophe elsewhere was to entrust the majority of dioceses in other Asiatic countries to a native clergy.

The efforts to build up a native clergy in India were by no means instituted recently, but they could not produce any great results, or be carried on extensively until the Roman Catholic educational system had been completely organized and young seminarists in general could receive a classical education. St Joseph's College at Tiruchirapally has now trained 900 native priests, some 200 of whom have entered the Society of Jesus. Many people will be surprised to learn that out of 5,575 Roman Catholic priests now active in India, 4,110 are Indians. Three-quarters of the clergy in India are men born in the sub-continent, and the percentage of native priests will no doubt soon increase, owing to the large number of Christian Indians who feel they have the vocation. At the moment there are some 2,000 students, mostly Indians, in the various seminaries, all fired with the intention of entering the priesthood. The flower of these are to be found at the Papal

Central Seminary in Poona. These, amounting to some 500, are coached in divinity by Jesuit teachers, and they can obtain the highest academic degrees at the seminary.

The 'Indianization' of the Church has developed south of the Bombay-Madras line to the extent that all dioceses there have bishops belonging to the national clergy. In the north they are still outnumbered by foreign missionaries, and the Church there continues to rely on priests of various nationalities sent out by Rome. Should this influx, as now appears likely, be stopped by the authorities, the Indian Church would become more and more dependent on the southern dioceses, who would then be expected to provide even more help than at present. What has happened with the secular priests is equally true for the religious Orders. There are today thousands of Indian Carmelites, Capuchins, Jesuits and so forth. Out of the 12,500 nuns working in the country, some 10,000 are already of Indian birth, and are mostly organized in national institutions.

During the last twenty years the picture presented by the Indian Church has fundamentally altered. The Roman Catholic Church has gone a long way to meet the new national aspirations of free India, or perhaps it would be better to say that she has anticipated them. Thus the Church in India has become a self-contained community, firmly attached to the land in which she has struck such deep roots. Whether the development of this new policy of the Church in India can be ascribed to the power of Indian nationalism consequent on her recently acquired political independence, or to the long-term threat of Communism, it is certainly in tune with the natural laws which govern the growth of a national Church; and it fulfils the ultimate aim of all missionary endeavour—namely, the creation of an indigenous, self-supporting Church, built on a sound foundation.

86. *In the streets of Bombay*

87. *Christians praying on the* maidan, *Bombay*

88. *Modern buildings on the Marine Drive, Bombay*

89. *Girl student in Indian dress*

90. *Indian Carmelite monk*

91. *Lecture in progress in the Jesuit seminary, Poona*

REGAL · TO-NIGHT
—SAVAGE DANGER!
—FABULOUS TREASURE!
—PRIMITIVE LOVE!
"STRANGE WORLD"
Actually Made in The NEVER-BEFORE-FILMED JUNGLES of the UNTAMED MATTO GROSSO!
STRANGE WORLD
ALEXANDER CARLOS
SEE!
SEE!
SEE! the
hunters of the
in berserk

87

88

90

91

Festivals of the Church in India

Four hundred years have elapsed since St Francis Xavier died in 1552, and his untouched earthly remains were exhumed from their sandy grave in the Chinese island of Sanzian and carried back in triumph to Goa. Ever since then the Indian Catholics have venerated his relics as sacred heirlooms. When we arrived in India pilgrims were streaming into Goa, where, on the occasion of the 400th anniversary of the death of St Francis, his relics were to be taken from the silver coffin, and publicly exhibited and adored by the people. The Indian Church desired to celebrate a sacred reunion with her apostle, and voice hymns of praise to the faith which he had preached. At the very moment when we arrived from Poona, a Portuguese ship carrying pilgrims reached Goa, and the whole of Panjim swarmed towards the harbour to greet the Papal Delegate, the Cardinal-Archbishop of Lisbon, who subsequently read his Papal Credentials to the assembled crowds, in front of Goa's principal church.

Thousands of pilgrims gathered in the Old Square of Goa on the following morning, December 3, the name day of St Francis Xavier. The faithful from all the Catholic centres of this enormous country (many of which we were to visit later) had converged on Goa. There were white-clad Christians from Malabar; Tamils from Madurai (who could easily be recognized by their multi-coloured clothes); fishermen and peasants from the villages of Goa; Goanese from Bombay, wearing European dress; and men of many other types and races, some even from distant Pakistan. The Adivasis of Chota Nagpur, too, were represented by a strong contingent. The whole of Roman Catholic India seemed to have assembled to give a lively and joyful demonstration of the development and the vitality of the great religious movement initiated by the saint. For that day, and several weeks afterwards, 'Golden Goa' woke from the deathlike sleep into which that forsaken and malaria-ridden city has lain for over a hundred years. The majority of the pilgrims camped in the shade of the palms which have now grown all over the extensive ruins of decaying houses. The wide corridors of St Monica's Convent, usually silent, were once more filled with nuns, the severe façade of Goa's mighty sixteenth-century cathedral gleamed in shimmering white brilliance, and in the Jesuit sanctuary of Bom Jesus a larger assembly of bishops and priests than Goa had ever seen in her whole history were gathered round the Jesuit Saint's silver shrine.

Punctually at nine o'clock the procession set out to carry the coffin into the cathedral. It was headed by members of the Brotherhoods from Goanese villages. Then came the various organized bands of pilgrims, and behind them walked hundreds of priests, twenty bishops, and the Cardinal-Legate. Finally came six archbishops, bearing on their shoulders the silver coffin containing the body of the saint.

The vast nave was not large enough to accommodate the huge crowds, who remained outside on the square, devoutly following the festival service which was relayed to them by wireless, as was also the message of the Holy Father in Rome. At the conclusion of High Mass the dignitaries of the Church walked towards the coffin which had been placed in the choir. The Patriarch of Goa, the Portuguese Governor and the Deacon of the Cathedral Chapter, each of whom had been given a key, opened the coffin, after which the Cardinal-Legate advanced, to be the first to adore the relics of the saint. Prelates, priests and distinguished persons followed him, and then, throughout that day and during several subsequent ones, thousands of pilgrims came in turn to worship at the shrine, sometimes standing for hours in the burning sun, praying and waiting patiently for the moment when they would be able to touch the saint's uncorrupted remains. Clad in priestly vestments, Francis Xavier rests on a sheet of ancient brocade. The features of his face are still clearly recognizable, though they have lost the life-like freshness which, according to trustworthy eye-witness reports, they still possessed 200 years after his death.

I stood for a long while beside the shrine and watched the devout manner in which the members of the Church of India, whether clerics or laymen, honoured their patron saint.

The coffin of St Francis Xavier had not yet been resealed when joyous news from Rome reached the Catholic Church of India. One of its members had been chosen by Pope Pius XII to be the first Indian Cardinal. The Holy Father's choice of Archbishop Valerian Gracias of Bombay, who was born in the little village of Navelim, near Goa, was so wise a selection that the Portuguese were also satisfied. On the last day of my stay in Christian India I was able to see the enthusiastic reception which the town of Bombay gave to its 'own' Cardinal. People had gathered in their hundreds of thousands on the superb *maidan* set in the heart of the city. Christians, Hindus, Mohammedans and Parsees were assembled there, and also officials of Church and State. Addressing people to whom noble birth and high rank means so much—in fact more than anything else—the new Cardinal made a touchingly modest speech, in which he admitted: "I am the son of a poor woman who could neither read nor write." He then referred to all the help which the Church had given him, and recalled the Swiss Jesuits whose school at Karachi he had attended, his Italian, German and Belgian teachers in the seminary, his patron, the then Portuguese Archbishop of Bombay;

94

95

CHURCH
DOMINE

97

98

and finally he spoke of his predecessor, Archbishop Roberts, a noble English Jesuit, who generously gave up his see to allow a son of India to take in his hands the Shepherd's Staff of the Church, and to become the religious leader of the first city in India.

Few lives could provide a better illustration than that of the new Cardinal of the selfless spirit in which the Church of Rome, ever since the days of Francis Xavier, has guided the Catholics of India; and of the inner transformation undergone by India herself in an epoch which has led a united and free nation to the threshold of a new era.

Those were my thoughts at the late hour, nearing midnight, when our aircraft took off from Indian soil. I cast a farewell glance at the millions of lights studding the area of the great city, before we flew into the deep darkness of the night, beyond which lay my distant homeland.

92. *Pilgrims in front of the Cathedral of St Catherine, Goa (sixteenth century)*

93. *Clergy and huge crowds assembled to receive the Papal Delegate in Panjim*

94. *Cardinal-Legate during the St Francis Xavier 400th anniversary celebrations in Goa*

95. *Opening the coffin of St Francis Xavier*

96. *The silver coffin of St Francis Xavier borne by six Archbishops to the Cathedral. On the left in front is Mgr Valerian Gracias, shortly afterwards appointed Cardinal Archbishop of Bombay*

97. *Indian nuns praying during the ceremony*

98. *Indian Catholics adoring the relics of the Saint*

99. *The procession of pilgrims in the Cathedral*

100. *Cardinal Archbishop Gracias making his entry into Bombay*